We are each so much more than
these uniforms we wear.

K. V. A.

praise for
ONWARD, AT LAST

"It is easy to feel hopeless in today's society and wonder just how we got here. Author Kevin Howard has answered this question for us and traced the corruption we have grown so accustomed to, back to one moment specifically. Kevin's words and ideas stick with the reader, providing hope for the somewhat hopeless future of America. People are craving a much-needed change, and Kevin takes it to the next step by not only pinpointing what changes can be made, but providing a framework for how such changes can be implemented. Kevin also provides a little history lesson along the way—that won't be found in US textbooks. The points made in, *Onward, At Last* will roll around in the reader's mind and make for great discussions around the dinner table."

– **Carolyn Jania, Narrator, Actress, Comedian**

"Kevin Howard is a commercial banker in his everyday life, but, within our universe, a deep thinker who questions the current state of American life in his new book, *Onward, At Last*. The concepts he introduces as solutions to our climate crisis, resource inequality, arms race, and technological disruption are easy to grasp and sensible. The book reads like a Thich Nhat Hanh Buddhist lecture disseminating powerful messages with grace, thoughtfulness, and slow breaths; no forceful commentary with anarchist tendencies or academic bullying. Mr. Howard found a new paradigm for rethinking our way of life to avoid an Orwellian outcome."

– **Joel Minamide, Commercial Banker,
Business Owner, Jazz Musician**

"Outstanding read! Glimpses into the new emerging paradigm. If you are distressed by all the signs of division, chaos, gloom and doom that are swirling about us, this book will help define the root causes of our collective malaise and offer the strands of hope that we can access to create a healthier future. Our current systems, built on the foundation of self-interest, competition, and privilege are no longer viable in a world that is struggling to realize its oneness. Our divisions into 'us' and 'them' may have been less toxic in the past before travel, communications, and global crises were less intrusive. Now all the negative fallout of a fragmented worldview—global warming, environmental catastrophes, fanaticism, toxic nationalism, offensive wealth inequality, war and brutality—are all combining to create an existential crisis for us all. Our current systems are bankrupt and crumbling one by one.

But there is hope. The author diagnoses the root causes of our malaise by explaining complex processes in understandable language and makes the convincing argument that the 'American dream' is an illusion that is no longer conducive to happiness and prosperity. He gives us a vision of a more loving and harmonious future that we can bring about by changing the way we think, by recognizing that our personal happiness is dependent on the fulfillment of all of us. He skillfully helps us to understand that by shifting our awareness, we can embrace who we truly are—each a cherished member of one human family."

– May Khadem, Ophthalmologist, Philanthropist

ONWARD, AT LAST

ONWARD, AT LAST

Kevin Howard

atmosphere press

*To Joyful...*you inspired me to write and so I have.

Table of Contents

Volume 3 – Mirror to the Way Forward

Volume 4 – Out of the Ashes of a Pandemic

Volume 5 – Impetus to a New Paradigm

Prologue

How did we arrive at a time where we know something is deeply wrong with our society and yet have no idea what it is or how to fix it? What can I do when everything seems too big to change?

These commentaries attempt to illuminate our current condition so each of us can choose our next step forward.

MY PROPOSITION
The values framing our choices are instilled in us through the relentlessly repetitious expressions of our native culture. In America, we hold these values of independence, competition, and self-interest so deeply that we hardly notice how they drive our choices, relationships, outlook, and world view. Yet, at a time when few of us are fulfilled, regardless of our wealth or privilege, what if the barrier to our happiness is our own core values?

This is the primary claim of *Onward, At Last...*

BOOK NOTE:
This book is organized in short, stand-alone commentaries that can be read in any order. The intent is to encourage your thoughtful consideration after you read each commentary. In order to facilitate your exploration beyond the ordered volumes, a category index has been included to group the com-

mentaries by the following topics: current events, economics, personal growth, politics, social evolution, and spirituality.

A COMMENT ON AUTHORITY/CREDENTIALS:
I do not write from a position of authority. I live and breathe just like you live and breathe. I am a talented, educated person, but this is not the basis on which I hope you will accept the validity of my commentaries. My intention is for you to measure the truth of my commentaries based on how they are validated by your actual experience. This is the most authentic way to ascertain the truth. The days of credentials validating truth are long passed.

Onward, At Last is a part of my ongoing commentaries regarding the way forward. Please feel free to join the conversation at my blog:

https://theuniversalonenessblog.com

Kevin V. Howard
a.k.a. AZStranger

VOLUME 1

Our Universal Oneness

The Universal Oneness Manifesto

We all came from the same place...

And we all will go to the same place.

The only distortion of our reality is our wide acceptance of our independence...our individuality...our inherent separateness.

From this mythology, all inhumanity is born.

A Simple Proposition

Intimacy is a clue to our universal oneness. By intimacy, I mean physical proximity. Consider the term "personal space," loosely defined as the physical comfort zone between ourselves and anyone else. Take into account how this personal space varies based on the relationship we have with individual people. The more we trust someone, the smaller our need for personal space becomes. On rare occasions, our personal space becomes synonymous with another person...and we no longer are separate people. We actually feel the other person. We hurt because they hurt. We feel joy because they are happy. We feel lonely when they are not present and complete when they are with us. Yet whoever this rare person is, they once were a complete stranger. The experience I describe is not unique...it is all too rare, fleeting, but pervasively true.

The question this truth reveals is whether the separateness we experience from strangers is true or just a widely accepted illusion? Context is another clue to answering this question. What makes a person a stranger is the cultural assumption they are driven by their own interest, guided by values of their own choosing, with no inherent responsibility to provide us with any consideration. Such a person cannot be trusted without knowing more. Therefore, when dealing with strangers, our need for personal space is at its maximum.

Now contrast this generic stranger with the litany of strangers we see on the evening news. Seeing something tragic or wonderful happening to a stranger on our TV screen can invoke very powerful emotions within us, depending on how we relate to this complete stranger. These feelings come from the same place as the emotions that join us with people we trust. They, too, are all too rare, fleeting, and pervasively true.

All that remains are the strangers we don't relate to...or do we? Who among us doesn't cherish the air we breathe? Or the water we drink? Or the warmth we feel when sheltered against the elements of our environment? What stranger can you imagine that doesn't seek safety and comfort for themselves and their families? Who doesn't have high aspirations for their children to live more fulfilling lives than they did?

We are one humanity because at the heart of this life, even at the moment of apparent individuality, our deepest hopes and aspirations are synonymous.

What Divides Us?

Let us consider our organizing American characteristics: independence, ordered liberty, self-interest, free-market economics, and currency as a medium of exchange. Each of these characteristics encourages differentiating individuals from each other.

As an independent person, I am free to choose my own values. My liberty is only limited by laws designed to prevent me from imposing on the liberty of other people.

At the heart of free-market economics is the utilitarian principle of individual actors making market choices based on their individual preferences (self-interest). Based on these choices, market prices are set for all goods and services in the global economy, thereby distinguishing consumers by their capacity to pay.

Accordingly, the quality of every good and service we buy is tied to how much money we have. Since most consumers cannot afford the very best quality goods and services, fortunes are made selling substandard quality to the broadest part of the market (i.e., Walmart).

Under these circumstances, well-being has become a function of fierce competition to accumulate money. As a consequence, the universal desire to provide for ourselves and our families is reduced to a zero-sum aspiration of inhuman, non-sustainable inequality.

What is this thing called Truth?

Truth is a complex concept because it is not limited to objective facts. Truth has a subjective component that accommodates anomalies, diverse worldviews, issues of faith, psychology, and much more.

In order to distinguish truth from myth, confirmation is necessary.

Accordingly, truth is a phenomenon that informs us...adds to our body of knowledge...forms the foundation for usable concepts...has application to our lives...is verifiable or at least confirmed by actual experience.

Truth provides meaning to our experiences and deepens our understanding of our lives and the world around us.

The cautionary tale about truth is it is distinct from goodness, decency, or convenience. Truth can be cruel. Yet no matter how truth affects us, we are invariably made better by knowing the truth because we are closer to the reality defining our lives.

This is why we must seek the truth. We need to be open to the truth wherever it exists. It behooves us to set aside our differences in order to be receptive to the truth.

As we consider our current political and social discourse, our greatest challenge to finding solutions is our unwillingness to be open to the truth regardless of the source.

Thankfully, we are all truth seekers. Let that be your starting point to finding the truth in your life.

Our Religious Isolation Is Another Myth

One of the unique characteristics of the three great religious traditions of Judaism, Christianity, and Islam is the broadly held belief that each offers the singular path to spiritual truth. Even in the name ascribed to the Creator: Adonai, God (Father, Son, Jesus Christ, and Holy Spirit), or Allah, is indigenous to each particular religious faith. Yet concurrent with the notion of one specific path to spiritual truth, the faithful subscribe to the foundational belief in a universal, all-powerful, all-knowing Creator. As a man raised in the Christian faith, and a deep reader of the scripture, I have become acutely aware of how religious practice sometimes differs from scriptural guidance.

One of the most important examples is the interpretation of Jesus Christ as the "narrow gate." At the heart of the Christian faith is the belief that Jesus died so all of our sins would be forgiven, and He rose from the dead to demonstrate our salvation. The significance of the universal forgiveness of sins was to allow all people to worship God (The Creator) directly. Therefore, Jesus was the "narrow gate" to our reconciliation with the Creator. As a result, the narrow gate has become the basis of Christian exclusivity for spiritual truth.

In Judaism, the tradition of the Chosen People includes the opportunity to sense Adonai's closeness, hear the truth, and share the truth with the world. Jewish salvation emphasizes correct conduct as revealed by the Mosaic covenant and recorded in the Torah and Talmud.

Islam is strictly monotheistic. A Muslim must earn her salvation by abiding by the Articles of Faith and actively practicing the Pillars of Faith, as prescribed by the Quran. Accordingly, each of these great religious traditions has expressed its exclusive claim for spiritual truth enforced by political and legal force and often violent conflict.

As a Christian, I look to the scriptural guidance regarding "speaking in tongues" to counter the tradition of Christian exclusivity of spiritual truth. The scripture introduced the practice of speaking in tongues to describe how, through the power of God, the Holy Spirit, we each hear the voice of God in our native tongue. To me, these verses of scripture epitomize the universality of an all-powerful Creator...one voice, vividly understood by all because the words are heard in the native tongue of the listener. This, in my view, is how a Universal Creator would speak, so all creation would understand. I further interpret the native tongue as a metaphor for the path each of us takes to discover our spiritual truth.

Assuming for a moment the presence of a Universal Creator, would our relationship be constrained by the randomness of birth?

I was born in the Bronx, New York. Would I have been raised in the Christian faith had I been born in Tehran? Or as a member of the Australian Aboriginal communities?

Doubtful.

Even as a practical matter, spiritual exclusivity feels more like ego than truth.

Why would I think that my narrow path to truth defines anyone else's path to truth? The full richness of our human experience teaches us of the boundless diversity of tangible, emotional, and spiritual reality.

Yet, at our core, who among us doesn't seek truth, confirmed by experience, which leads to a deeper purpose for living?

The Symbol of our Oneness
is in your Hands

Take a look at your hands. Ten fingers attached to two palms...
each with unique functions, capable of moving independently
or in concert with each other. Think of each of us as the fingers
and our Earth as the palms.

Now consider our independence...our individual liberty...
our inalienable right to advance our own interests. How we
express our liberty through individual choices shapes the lives
we live, the careers we have, and the families we form. But are
we actually independent?

Most of us don't produce our food, build our homes, or
provide the protection that secures ourselves and our loved
ones. We all rely on others to provide the education and skill
development necessary to succeed in the vocations of our
choice. Still, others provided the roads, highways, bridges,
water systems, electric grid systems, and communications
systems necessary to function in modern society. In fact, as
individuals, we contribute very little to the components that
provide for our living conditions. Yet we still reserve upon
ourselves the right to advance our own self-interest, even to
the detriment of the people and resources we rely on to live.

We have one planet that produces and replenishes a finite
amount of resources. All of us rely on these resources to
provide the living conditions we enjoy. Under our current
economy, we access these finite resources based on the

amount of money we possess. For those few people who possess enormous amounts of money, control over the lion's share of our global resources is in their hands. They alone retain the right to exhaust these resources or utilize them in a sustainable way. We are experiencing their decisions playing out in the Climate Change debate.

The question for the rest of us is simple: If global temperatures rise as predicted, unabated by fossil fuel utilization, can life as we know it exist for long? Globally confirmed scientific observations say no. Yet the reason scientific evidence is not determining our only rational choice is that fortunes built on the use of fossil fuels are being deployed to hinder the global transition to a net-zero carbon future. This illuminates the danger of self-interest. Does it make sense to define individual liberty within the context of self-interest when our preservation relies on advancing our common interest? The answer is obvious when you look at your hands again. Can the fingers survive without the palms?

Scarcity in All things but One

The one characteristic that defines our lives is scarcity. None of us has enough money, time, health, opportunity, satisfaction, fulfillment, etc. Yet of all these scarce resources, the one we have in boundless abundance is LOVE.

I know none of us receives as much love as we want, but our capacity to give love is limitless. Have you ever considered that none of us receive all the love we want because none of us gives all the love we can? Culturally speaking, we treat love like it is the rarest treasure. And as a result, we reserve it for only the most deserving people.

But what if we have real reasons to love more broadly? What if love in its purest form is simply the joy we feel from bringing happiness to others who make our lives worth living?

The culmination of human experience has provided the society, technology, culture, social mores, virtues, and critical lessons that we benefit from every day. Our contemporaries provide every aspect of our lives we are incapable of providing for ourselves. Our very existence remains a function of choices people we will never know make each and every day. Yet somehow, we are able to go on each day as if we are primarily responsible for our own well-being.

The time is long past for us to realize a fellow human installed the brakes on our car, found the flaw in our aircraft, caught the assailant who meant us harm, paved the way for our success, introduced us to our spouses, yielded in rush hour traffic when we desperately had to get home, and found the way to serve our food, despite the sick child they have at home.

Contrary to conventional wisdom, we are immersed in a world of many people fully deserving of our love.

All we need to do is stop thinking of ourselves and notice.

My North Rim experience...

I have dreamed about going to the North Rim of the Grand Canyon for years. I have been to the more frequented South Rim multiple times and had the pleasure of hiking to Havasupai Falls and camping for four days. Every time I travel to the Grand Canyon, I am renewed by the natural, majestic beauty of our functioning ecology. Imagine the vivid night sky unimpeded by the light pollution of modern city life...darkness filled with bright, distant beacons sparkling like diamonds. I longed for the renewal that has only come when I am immersed in the most natural settings. I have been here for one day. The North Rim's beauty is beyond written description. Yet the renewal I hoped for will not come.

Why? The sky is blotted with a haze of chemtrails. What would otherwise be a gorgeous clear-to-naturally cloudy sky has been reduced to a haze of industrial manipulation. As I look in the sky, a relentless series of planes fly above the Canyon, leaving massive Xs across the sky. This expanding image reminds me of America's successful moon landing, where our astronauts left an American flag planted on the surface. Then...we claimed the moon. Today... "they" claim the sky.

Historically, we claim the earth through the ownership of her land, water, and natural resources. But who are we to claim any of it? What did we do to think we have the right to control nature's resources for our own exclusive uses? Even here at the remote North Rim of the Grand Canyon, we dare to claim the sky and use it for whatever undisclosed purpose... robbing everyone else of enjoying the natural beauty of this otherwise pristine setting. Thankfully, this is the last throw of the old paradigm. Self-interest has run its course.

More and more people see the destructive effects of unbridled self-interest. We are hitting critical mass in social, political, economic, and spiritual thought, where people acknowledge our interdependence on each other and the natural environment that provides for our survival. This new realization is elevating the shift toward common interest as a core consideration. Sustainability and efficient utilization of resources will be the new currency. Waste, gluttony, and degradation will be the primary forbidden vices. Compared to the old paradigm, critics will accuse us of seeking Utopia. We do not. We are evolving out of necessity. And like every species of life, we will adjust or manifest our own extinction.

Why Love matters

Has time ever stopped for you?

Your mind was quiet. What was next didn't matter. You even forgot where you were. And for a moment, you almost felt boundless.

It didn't have to be a romantic moment. It could have happened anywhere. The one compelling feature was the capture of at least one of your senses. But in that moment, you felt connected to someone...to something...and in that instant, nothing else mattered.

Then life began again. The noise returned. Yesterday defined tomorrow without consideration for today. And the serenity you felt in that instant receded just beyond your reach.

Modernity deceives us into believing...doing breeds fulfillment. Yet actual experience teaches us... being provides our ultimate satisfaction. Consider the last time you felt abundant fulfillment. Regardless of the reasons that led to your best experiences, you only realized them once you stopped and let them soak all the way in.

In that moment, you felt love. There is no happier feeling than when we suspend our busy lives and connect with the world that surrounds us.

Inversely, every other moment is defined by our preternatural loneliness, disguised as boredom, listlessness, or anxiety...

We are all North Koreans these days

...worshipping on the altar of our "Divine Leaders." Who is your Kim Jong-un? Mine has been Jesus Christ. Some submit to Adonai, Allah, Buddha, the natural Universe...still others to science or a trusted source of information that defines our world view.

Regardless of the target of our devotion, we are called to give absolute fealty...to take as unimpeachable truth any perceived pronouncements from the altar...to form monolithic associations with other true believers (Us), and to offer scorn and contempt to anyone who dares to hold different beliefs (Them).

Be rest assured, there are millions of fellow human beings in North Korea today who are certain of our damnation for not yielding to the commands of their "divine leader." If any of us are completely honest, their certainty will feel very familiar. This is the heart of everything wrong with life today. For people like "Us," "we hold these truths to be self-evident that all men are created equal."* And for people like "Them," they deserve the inhumanity we provide because they don't share our values.

Have you noticed there are fewer of Us these days and far too many of Them? Truly faithful versus falsely faithful; Faithful versus non-faithful; Objective versus subjective; True

---

* Thomas Jefferson

Americans versus Fake Americans; Americans versus Foreigners; Conservatives versus Liberals; Democrats versus Republicans; Allies versus Axis of Evil; *Fox News* versus *MSNBC*; *NY Times* versus Infowars; GMO versus Organic; Renewable energy versus Oil/Coal; An Inconvenient Truth versus Global Warming Deniers...

Yet while we condemn Them, have we considered but for the randomness of birth, we would be them?

None of us choose our place of origin, but where we are born, the family that raises us, and the culture we are given all frame our choice of values. Acknowledging how we became so certain of our beliefs should illuminate how they became certain of theirs.

The moment we can see our choices in their eyes is the instant we connect to our mutual humanity.

Today, we are all North Koreans.

The moment the nightmare ends

Each night as I close my eyes, I leave behind the concerns of the day. I suspend reality as I submit to the blissful recharge of a good night's sleep. As thoughts of the day recede, a new subconscious reality emerges. Here, I realign my conscious and subconscious identity by hearing the message of unspoken truth.

This morning, the question I awoke to is, "how do we get to a place where our values undermine our humanity?" I arrived here by separation alone. From the moment my self-view starts and ends with "I," my consciousness detaches from my humanity.

A worldview seen through the prism of "I" encourages self-preservation at the expense of anyone else.

From birth, I was taught to think this way. I loved anyone who fed me, who cleaned me, who comforted me. As I grew older, I learned to distrust other people because they were not inclined to make me comfortable. They want and need what I want and need, but I was taught there is not enough for both of us. Consequently, I cultivate personal alliances of mutual self-service and work to provide the resources that secure us.

Fortified by the virtues of individual liberty and the pursuit of my own happiness, I am encouraged to take for myself and my alliance all the resources I can. To save and protect my accumulating resources for myself and the few who make me comfortable. I rationalize that I earned my mountain of resources; therefore, I deserve the privilege of keeping them for myself.

The great irony here is gluttony breeds emptiness. The more I accumulate, the more detached I become.

And so, sleep brings a promise of relief, only to reveal what I was told is a lie.

I did not create myself. I did not raise myself. I did not teach myself. I do not feed myself. Any fulfillment I experience is inspired by my interactions with humanity and the natural environment that sustains me.

The dissonance pervading my life is the virtue of an "I" centered worldview, at odds with the reality of my existence.

I am part of one humanity. I am fed by my connection with humanity. As we prosper, I prosper. And as humanity suffers, I suffer. Up to this moment, I lived a life of serving myself and my alliance at the expense of humanity.

Today, I finally awoke from my nightmare.

When time stops...

...my pace slows.

My breath deepens.

Awareness sharpens.

In this moment, I learn so much more about who I am... where I am...why now matters.

For the first five decades of my life, I never experienced this depth of my reality. As if I spent my youth skimming the surface of life, I now am immersed in the richness of an increasingly vivid consciousness.

What am I learning?

The upper currents of life demand conformity, while the lower currents encourage free awareness, self-actualization, and clarity. I surmise the upper currents are crowded because that's where most of us live. Conformity becomes necessary for movement to be possible.

But as I slow to the deeper currents, I'm free. Free to breathe slowly and deeply. To notice the subtle and the vivid. And the deeper I travel in this very moment, the more connected I feel to humanity, nature, and eternity.

Still waters do run deep.

Find your stillness, and you will discover your nirvana.

Life Demystified

Death...
An ending.
A beginning.
A continuation of sentience transformed.
A restoration of our universality.
The last lesson of our experience set.
Yes. No. Maybe.

Birth
An end of gestation.
A new beginning.
A continuation of sentience transformed.
An illusionary separation from our universality.
The first lesson of our experience set.
Yes. No. Maybe.

Eternity
Infinity
Universality
Divine...
...Our most fundamental condition.

Contrast is stimulating, illuminating, and contextualizing;
And once understood, forever beautifying.
So live. Feel. Die. Restore.

One Breath

Life at its simplest, most basic level can be understood with one breath cycle.

As we inhale, our lungs are filled with the air we need. Oxygen is distributed by our circulatory system to all areas of our body. Our bodies warm, and we feel the momentary benefit of our basic need satisfied.

Then the moment passes...and we begin to exhale.

The oxygen we need is getting used and simultaneously converted to carbon dioxide...a substance we need to release.

As the carbon dioxide leaves our body, the feeling of relief is palpable...ultimately culminating in a moment of serene contentment.

This moment is the epiphany revealed most completely by meditation.

Here we get a temporary glimpse of the euphoria we will experience when we no longer live.

Then the moment recedes...as we are consumed with the need to inhale once again.

Who we are

Height, width, depth...3rd dimension

Duration, mortality, the ever-ticking clock...4th dimension

Transcendence, eternal, infinite perception...5th dimension

Collective consciousness, Divinity, Universal Oneness...6th dimension

Multiverse, Surreality, beyond perception...7th dimension

Like the caterpillar in the cocoon, we ascend to the next higher reality. And with each transition, we are challenged to remember who we are.

VOLUME 2

Interdependence

Where from here?

I have deep empathy for the realization that political affiliation is pointless in a system of rigged election processes and mass disinformation. In my view, the underlying cause is our American values. The highest aspiration of American life is to achieve financial independence...to perfect the practice of accumulating wealth for ourselves. Like most phenomena, self-interest and free-market capitalism works within an effective range of activity and fails to work as intended beyond that range.

Historically, the institutions of government and the media had facilitated necessary corrections when concentrations of wealth and power exceeded the effective range. Over the last 45 years (Google "Lewis Powell memo"), the investment class contributed a material portion of their earnings to co-opt universities (research for commerce over scholarship), government (lobbying and Supreme Court packing – Powell was appointed to the Supreme Court by President Nixon in 1972), and media (conversion of news independent of entertainment to news as entertainment – spin over information) to prevent the correction that would have happened after the financial crash of 2008. Consequently, the Obama recovery locked in severe financial inequality, effectively accelerating the already dangerous siphoning of income from working-class and middle-class Americans.

In the absence of healthy institutions, we, the People, are all that is left to bring about the change we need. While much has been written about the need for us to look past the divisiveness that distracts us, I encourage our search to go deeper to challenge the values we hold as truth.

The investment class is advancing their interests by any means necessary, which encourages each of us to do the same. We must resist this urge and come to the realization that the best way to advance our self-interest is to fully serve and support our common interest.

It is a fact of modern life that we as individuals survive and thrive primarily based on the actions of other people. The interdependence of humanity is our defining strength. We cannot reach the full potential of our physical, emotional, and spiritual selves if we don't honor our natural interdependence on each other.

This is the way forward.

Who Built this Anyway?

I didn't.

I contributed. I worked hard to acquire the best education possible. Yet, virtually everything I know was first developed by someone else and taught to me by someone else.

Today, I'm a talented, experienced small business banker. I still remember the person who hired me in my first position as a Disaster Assistance Loan Officer for FEMA. I remember each person who hired me for each position I held thereafter, including the one I hold now.

The most impactful contributors to my career have been the borrowers who came to me for the financing they needed to rebuild their lives or achieve their goals.

I vividly recall the schoolteacher who lost his home and most of his possessions due to devastating floods that hit southern Georgia in 1994. He and his wife had been married for a few years and were expecting their first child. They had invested all of their savings into their modest home. There was no way on a teacher's salary they could afford to rebuild their home and pay the existing mortgage. The Disaster Assistance Program offered a 30-year mortgage at the government's cost (30 years fixed at 4 percent vs. market rates of 10 percent) that financed the total reconstruction of the home, refinanced the existing mortgage, and replaced the destroyed personal property, all for less than the original mortgage payment. I was able to approve an exception to the policy to lower their final payment because their original mortgage payment was half of their monthly earnings. When I told the borrower what I was able to approve, he cried. I'm crying now just thinking about it.

In 2015, I had a borrower who came to me for financing to buy five Domino's Pizza franchises in Arkansas. The borrower had no significant collateral to secure the loan, but was offering his life's savings as the down payment. This borrower had started working at one of the Domino's stores as a pizza delivery man twenty years ago. He worked his way up to shift manager, then store manager, then larger store manager, and finally general manager of all five stores. The franchise owner was retiring and wanted to sell his stores to his best employee. I never met this borrower in person, and he never met me. But people like him are why I became a banker. His was the proudest loan of my career.

No, I didn't build this.

All the people who paved the way for me; All the people who taught me; All the people who believed in me; All the people who hired me; And all the borrowers who gave me the opportunity to provide financing...together, we built this.

A Human life is a terrible thing to waste

Beyond life's few certainties, death and taxes, reside the space for spiritual and emotional growth that offers each of us the opportunity to find fulfillment.

At the moment of our conception, our nature is hard-wired with a wide range of physical inclinations that manifest based on the nurture we receive. Optimally, we incubate for forty weeks, where we transform into a life ready to function separate from our womb. Our development is a function of our mother's physical and emotional well-being...her access to proper shelter, healthy nutrition, exposure to toxins, physical and emotional stress, and prenatal care. We reach the first stage of our full potential when we are born as a healthy, fully formed baby.

In our infancy, our genetic inclinations are cultivated based on an intricate, intimate web of emotional and physical relationships. Our developmental security is achieved through the formation of an external womb, commonly known as a family. Here we experience emotional clarity: we are fulfilled when our personal space is synonymous with our family; Otherwise, we are miserable.

During our toddler stage, we are introduced to societal norms...familial roles, culture, personal space, and social mores. Here our family prepares us for a second birth, into the world beyond the family. This second stage ends as we embark on our formal education.

Our educational stage, typically in the US from the age of 5 through 18 and beyond, provides the physical, emotional, and spiritual foundation of our personal development. Here we get the first glimpse of who we are and how we connect to the world around us. We are exposed to the lessons of history and are provided our first opportunity to internalize those lessons for application in our daily lives. Our full potential is achieved at this third stage when we enter adulthood as physically, emotionally, and spiritually healthy people, fully empowered to contribute to the broader society.

Our baseline expectations are set. The range of career opportunities is framed for primary selection. We are expected to make the choices that will shape the rest of our lives. The core question is, how many of us are fully prepared when our critical choices must be made? What are the consequences if we are not ready?

This is where so many of us learn the cruel reality of modern life. Our baseline expectations of building a life that provides security for ourselves and our families are all too often exposed as a romantic notion when faced with free-market competition. Rarely is the competition free or fair.

We put our heads down and work like mules in the hopes of earning our way to our dream life. Five, ten years go by, and we meet a person who brings us glimpses of happiness. We get married. Now our desire to find security becomes more urgent because it is not just us anymore. Dreams of a life of fulfillment fade into distant memories behind a busy array of tasks and responsibilities.

Why is modern life not more fulfilling today? We have

simply exchanged spending most of our time producing what we need to survive with spending most of our time earning the money to survive. Given all the technological advances and the abundance of natural resources, we now have the capability to provide all of humanity with the resources each of us can use to reach our full potential.

What stands in our way? A system of economics that encourages us to take unto ourselves as much as we can. A value structure that indoctrinates us into believing we are separate, independent, self-interested individuals who can expect only what we earn in life.

Yet, who among us earned the mother's womb that gave us life? Or the years of nurturing provided by our families? Or the countless lessons provided by teachers, mentors, family, and friends? In fact, who among us earned the love we receive?

We have known since Copernicus that we are not at the center of the universe. The lesson here is we are part of the universe. We are individual members of one humanity who share one planet. Each of us is vitally important because we possess enormous potential to contribute to our communities.

Even so, how many young adults today are empowered to reach their full potential? How many are sufficiently informed to master their highest vocational aspirations? Almost none when compared to our global population.

Up to this moment, even in the richest country on Earth, almost all people live their entire lives working jobs they otherwise would not do but for the need to make money. For a while, the desire for money can generate high productivity, but before long diminishing returns set in. Work, no matter how lucrative, becomes a daily grind, leaving us empty and unfulfilled. The lesson here is that fulfillment is the ultimate inspiration for productivity. To do daily what you feel most passionate about is the fuel that is forever sustainable.

The next step of our social evolution is to align our values with the wisdom of our human experience. E pluribus Unum... out of many, one. Each of us, no matter where we live, is too valuable to waste. None of us, no matter our privilege, can survive without the rest of us. Therefore, we best advance our individual well-being by empowering each other to reach our full potential.

Out with the Old; In with the New

Do we really require human deprivation in order to feel special?

What if we can enjoy all the pleasures of privilege without subjugating others?

The key is removing the need for accumulation by guaranteeing everyone has access to the resources they can use to reach their full potential.

Consider dinner at home with your family. No one lunges at the food with the intent to take as much as they can, because everyone knows they are guaranteed to get their full share.

In this emerging new society, waste is the primary vice that virtue must eradicate. Prestige is tied to how much we each contribute to the well-being of humanity. Human progress will accelerate based on unleashing our individual potential.

If my proposition sounds too lofty for your sensibilities, you remain constrained by the old paradigm...scarcity. Let me be blunt. Scarcity is caused by the incentive to accumulate, which is necessary when you are not guaranteed access to resources. This old paradigm has proven to be unsustainable.

Faced with mass migration induced by resource deprivation, resource hoarding societies will either impose apartheid-style immigration policies or experience unmanageable population growth.

Thankfully, a new alternative is emerging: a full-access, resource management-based, global economy. Yet, for this well-documented alternative to be viable, each of us must reconsider our values. How do we best advance the well-being of ourselves and our families? By maximizing the ability of every person to contribute to our global well-being.

My Declaration of Interdependence

At the founding of America, the forefathers declared independence from British rule because King George III practiced tyranny over the American colonies. In organizing the new nation, the fundamental rights of free people were acknowledged in the Bill of Rights, which defined our individual autonomy with the principle of ordered liberty. In practice, the concept of ordered liberty, which empowers the government to limit our freedom where it impermissibly limits the freedom of others, has translated to freedom to advance our self-interest. Each of these events occurred within the context of economic modernization.

As societies progressed from hunter-gatherers to agrarian, to industrial, to post-industrial, to information-based models, we improved productivity and accelerated innovation through specialization. The sum effect of modernity is rapid improvement in life expectancy and many other quality of life measures in exchange for a growing, yet hardly acknowledged, interdependence on humanity.

Interdependence involves mutual dependence for mutual benefit. Each of us exchanges the excess productivity of our specialized skills for the remainder of the goods and services that sustain us. Interdependence is distinguished from codependency, a condition involving the dependence of one party, often for the benefit of an enabling party.

In our modern society, we use money as a medium of

exchange for our specialized skills. As such, money is the necessary condition for accessing all goods and services, including the development of specialized skills. By limiting access to skill development based on how much money we have, modern societies create a global caste of under-skilled people who are codependent on wealthy benefactors. This condition is not sustainable because the benefits are not mutual.

The first step toward a sustainable, mutually fulfilling, interdependent society is acknowledging the benefit each of us receives is tied to the ability of all of us to contribute.

The quality of the food we eat is tied to the well-being of the people who produce it.

The quality of the shelter we enjoy is tied to the well-being of the people who built it.

The quality of love we receive is tied to the well-being of the people who provide it.

My well-being is tied to the well-being of every person who contributes to the conditions that sustain me.

Therefore, I gladly declare my interdependence on humanity, and I commit to supporting policies that advance the well-being of all of us.

I am...You are...We Do.

I matter.

You matter.

Each of us offers our unique perspective on the reality we experience.

Each of us contributes individually to our society.

Our individuality is the prism that translates our experiences and ultimately defines how we choose to connect to reality.

But our individuality is not enough for survival.

To survive, we rely on many other individuals, past and present, to provide the knowledge, thoughtful discretion, productivity, and resource management to maintain the environment that supports daily living.

While experience teaches few truths are absolute, human interdependence informed by individual ingenuity is the essential truth of our existence.

Therefore, I matter, and You matter, but only WE will do...for us to prosper.

Finding Purpose in a Cacophony of Inhumanity

Here we are immersed in the white noise of 24/7 news chatter...real news commingled with fake news. Who has time to suspend the grind of our own lives to tell the difference? So we turn to alternative sources...the internet blogs, more white noise laced with relentless rants designed to undermine the last shred of faith we have in any mainstream news source, politician, or public institution. Is there no end to the noise? When did we forget how to talk about our challenges and concerns without yelling past each other?

Time for each of us to take a deep breath and pause for a moment. Repeat the deep breathing until the noise fades away. Now that you have created a moment of calm, allow one question to enter your consciousness:

How do we as a humanity evolve beyond our current dilemma?

I acknowledge the enormity of the problem is paralyzing. The fact that any necessary change will take many years, and likely last beyond our lifetimes, only makes the problem intractable. But for the sake of our progeny and our sanity, we must do something.

Where do we begin? Root causes. The root cause of any problem strips the litany of false leads & convenient scapegoats and reveals how we find ourselves here.

Our problem is systemic scarcity. Today, countless people

are starving while we throw away millions of pounds of food. Millions suffer and die from treatable diseases while thousands of available hospital beds lay empty. Billions of people live a century behind modern knowledge and technology, denying most of them the opportunity to discover their full potential. Virtually every person spends most of their lives toiling away at jobs they would never do but for the need for money.

In a world of resource abundance, how did access to resources become so limited? A system of social organization and economics where access to resources is tied to how much money you have. Since only money guarantees access, each of us is encouraged to accumulate as much money as possible. The result is a world where most of the global wealth is consolidated in very few hands, and half the world's population is severely resource-deprived.

If scarcity is our problem, the solution is to maximize human productivity by guaranteeing access to all the resources each of us can use to reach and maintain our full potential. By limiting consumption to what we can use, reducing waste by maximizing the quality of all goods and services, allowing all people full access to the accumulation of human knowledge, and leveraging the use of automation to eliminate the need for mundane, repetitive tasks for human labor, we create the conditions where each of us can achieve our full potential.

Is this solution possible? Yes, but only if we reconcile our defining values to the wisdom of our experience. Each of us relies on many people to produce the conditions that sustain us. As a result, our individual well-being is a function of the well-being of every person who contributes to our living conditions.

The farmer who grows our food and the truck driver who delivers it to market...the electrician who wires our home and the mechanic who installs our brake pads...the pilot who flies our plane and the engineers who designed it...the teacher who exposed us to our life's chosen vocation and every person who believed in us...Each and every one of these people and many more we may never know contribute to the conditions that make our lives worth living. And when they are distracted, undernourished, ailing, and denied access to the resources they need, we suffer from faulty goods and services that often alter the trajectory of our lives.

Once each of us acknowledges our interdependence on humanity, we realize we all must matter if we want to live in a sustainable, mutually fulfilling society.

How then do we get from here to there?

Helping each person we know to understand we can best advance our self-interest by supporting the well-being of all of us. Changing the dialogue of our public policy discussions from "how does policy affect me?" to "how does policy help us?" Supporting candidates and causes that favor global unity over nationalism and sectarianism. Doing the relentlessly hard work of building an emerging critical mass of values that elevates all of humanity.

This is the task at hand, which offers purpose amid a cacophony of inhumanity.

Why Loving You Doesn't Make Me
a Dreamer

I love you because...

You decided to have me.

You carried and nourished me in your body for forty weeks.

You taught me the language that expresses my thoughts and frames my dreams.

You raised me, educated me, believed in me long before I knew who I could be.

Your efforts, discoveries, and choices produced the body of knowledge I use daily to contribute to the world around me.

I am able to work because you paved the roads that lead to my job, built the car I drive, and completed all the repairs that allow my car to run.

You produce my food, my shelter, my safety, and every-thing I need that I am unable to produce for myself.

I do participate in my life, but compared to your contribution, my efforts seem nearly meaningless.

So yes...I love you. Because given all you do, loving you is the most rational, practical, and obvious thing I can do.

Quieting the Noise

The thing about figuring out the external problems that impact our lives is the scale is too big. Most people simply do not have the time or energy, beyond taking care of themselves and their families, to connect the dots. This is why the discussion invariably becomes white noise, because the problems appear intractable. The solution is to show how the choices each of us make contributes to the problems afflicting our lives.

We are all aware of the choices we make and possess the ability to make different choices if we see the benefit. So how do each of us contribute to the external problems impacting our lives? By making choices daily, framed by our values, which isolate us from the global community that provides for our well-being.

Starting with a basic acknowledgment of how we survive each day. Every person can look at their lives, review their own personal experiences, and see independence, freedom, self-interest, nationalism, and sectarianism are all self-defeating lies. Yet these are the virtues that define us as Americans. These values define our idea of success. Yet as we each work harder to chase "success," we find little fulfillment in either the journey or the destination.

The good news is this is a problem each of us can solve.

Don't fear, blame, hate, or hurt the hands that feed you.

Appreciating and honoring the hands that feed us allows us to be fulfilled by sustenance.

How did we make it this far...

...given all the challenges of our modern lives?

After all the ranting, blaming, and widespread scapegoating, we stand here poised to do something...anything, but what?

Experience has taught us that more venting is definitely not working. And disconnecting leaves us bearing the brunt of a dysfunctional society, with no hope of facilitating change.

Where do we go from here?

Like any good explorer, the way forward is tied to how we arrived here in the first place. Regardless of the path we have taken, all of us are survivors. We survive and even thrive because we have utilized the resources necessary to support our well-being. And the only precondition for the resources we rely on is countless people, supported by our natural environment, who successfully produced the needed goods and services we did not produce for ourselves. Let this sink into your consciousness while I dispense with a modern myth.

Money did not make this happen.

We all have spent money on goods and services that were inadequate or even detrimental to our well-being. While money is a necessary precondition for accessing resources, only high-quality, effective human innovation and effort, supported by our natural environment, provide the resources that actually support our well-being.

Once we acknowledge our daily well-being is a function of

the effective efforts of countless people, we realize both how we have survived thus far and how best to proceed.

Now consider how we make choices today. How often do we consider the countless people who contribute daily to our well-being? In fact, social norms encourage us to think only of ourselves and the people we love and to fear other people. The values that define American society support this outlook by teaching us we have a fundamental right to pursue our own happiness.

Yet despite being empowered to provide only for ourselves and our families, we find we are angry as hell because it is becoming increasingly hard to do. Why?

Because the wealthiest people, empowered by the right to pursue their own happiness, are taking an increasingly higher percentage of global resources for themselves. Ironically, since we believe pursuing our own happiness is a virtue, we would rather blame other resource-deprived people for our struggles. The culmination of our collective angst is America has put the world on notice. We will no longer allow the less wealthy countries of the world to take advantage of us anymore. This Orwellian rationalization is the path to dystopia.

Each of us has the power to expand the sphere of our consideration when we make choices. If it is an undeniable truth that we survive based on the effective efforts of countless people, then it is in our best interest to consider the general well-being of all people when we make choices that affect their lives.

Reconnecting to how we survived thus far is the guidepost for the path to sustainable well-being.

When our true north turns out to be true south...

...We find ourselves in a place we hardly recognize.

Feel familiar? Let us consider where we are.

We were raised to value our freedom above all else. Freedom to choose our faith, our career, whether to get married and have a family. Freedom to do with our time what we choose. Yet almost all of us spend our entire lives working jobs we would never do, but for the need for money. And for the very few of us who have accumulated enough money to reclaim our time for ourselves, what price did we have to pay? Did we sacrifice healthy relationships with our spouses and children? Or maybe just our basic humanity by being willing to make unthinkable choices for huge sums of cash?

What choices? Consider the fortunes made selling food that destroys the lives of their customers...or the money made deploying planned obsolescence that kills people due to intentional system failure...or the junk science paid for by vested interests to convince people prescription drugs cure diseases...or the countless marketing jingles that associate harmful products with our most cherished values or desires.

We were raised to value the pursuit of our own happiness as one of our most cherished fundamental rights. Now we address the most important public policy issues with a simple question: How is the policy going to affect me? Is there any wonder why we are incapable of solving critical problems facing our society?

We were raised to be independent people. To build a life that allows us to be as independent of other people as possible. Today, the Good Samaritan is a snowflake, and people needing help are labeled takers. Yet do any of us actually live independently? Do we produce our own food? Build our own shelter? Pave our own roads? Fight our own wars?

The fact is we grind through our daily lives guided by values that are not leading us to the fulfillment we sorely deserve. We have exhausted ourselves by blaming an endless list of others for our lack of fulfillment. In desperation, we turned to a carnival barker to lead us back out of the wilderness, only to realize he was the glitter that was most definitely not gold.

Where do we go from here?

Stop grinding. Stop digging. Stop running. Just stop, breathe deeply, then set aside the noise and expectations of our busy, modern lives. Find a mirror and take a moment to look at yourself. The answer to your fulfillment is staring back at you.

All fulfillment requires is an alignment of our physical, emotional, and spiritual lives. When our values inspire choices that serve our highest purpose, we feel the euphoria of fulfillment.

Today, our values have led us to a society we hardly recognize. And our aimless wandering will not end until we realize the compass that guides our journey is broken.

Independence from each other. Freedom of each other. Self-interest without consideration for each other...all lead to dystopia because our individual prosperity is a function of the constructive contributions of all of us.

We are one humanity, interdependently nourished by one natural universe.

This is the undeniable fact of our existence.

When our values are aligned with the physical requirements of our existence, we will make choices that serve our highest purpose.

Then, and only then, will we find the fulfillment we seek.

As Above...so below

Existence has a pattern that replicates from the smallest to the largest.

Consider our human body, which is comprised of over 30 trillion cells and includes about 200 different types of cells. Each type of cell possesses unique characteristics that allow it to perform a specialized function. Our bodies survive because each category of cells executes their unique functions in coordination with every other category of cells for the good of the whole body.

Consider how we use our bodies daily. We talk, walk, eat, drink, use our hands, and do many more common tasks. Each one of these functions requires the coordinated effort of several component parts, contributing very specialized skills in order to effectively complete the most basic task. For example, the act of grasping a cup of coffee in the morning is only possible because all five fingers, guided by the vision provided by our eyes, work together to secure the cup.

Consider how we function in our modern society. Each of us develops very specialized skills that we contribute in exchange for money, which allows us to purchase all the material requirements of life that we do not produce for ourselves. Imagine how many people are involved in producing our daily food, clean water, clothing, shelter, security, and even the beds we sleep in each night. Any one or group of these people who fail to provide good service can lead to very detrimental impacts on our lives. Understood this way, a good day occurs when many people acting in concert successfully complete their unique functions for our mutual benefit.

As complex of a miracle as our modern societies can be, we are unable to survive without the natural environment. Sunlight, water, oxygen, atmospheric pressure, biodiversity, and many other factors all combine to create the ecosystem we need to survive.

This is how we exist each day.

Take note of the pattern that produces our existence. Each individual contributor, internally and externally, work in coordination to create the conditions that support our daily physical wellness. The value of each contributor is not how we compare to each other, but where we stand in relation to making our maximum contribution for the good of all. **This is the virtue that illuminates our highest purpose.**

Yet, where do we stand?

We live in a society that honors independence, freedom, self-interest, and boundless individual accumulation of wealth obtained through competition.

While none of us choose the family or country of our birth, we are drafted into a lifetime of competition that determines our access to resources and range of skill development. More than half of the 7.9 billion humans on earth are so resource-deprived they rarely have the opportunity to reach their full potential. Even for the wealthiest 11 percent of humanity living in the United States, Canada, and the European Union, significant parts of the population lose the birth lottery and are denied full access to the resources needed to reach their full potential.

At what cost?

Imagine the explosion of human potential, innovation, creativity, and productivity if all people were able to access the accumulation of human knowledge? Yet this immeasurable human potential is lost on the altar of competition, which is neither free nor fair. The price we pay is a profound degradation of human development.

Yet we still have a choice.

We can learn the lessons of how we exist. We can take note of the role each component part plays on the whole. We can acknowledge our purpose is tied to the application of our unique talents, contributed for the good of all of us. We will then be free to commit our lives to serving our highest purpose.

And the moment we do, we will find the fulfillment that has eluded us for so long.

You Are a Part of Me I Do Not Yet Know

Sounds utopian...I know, but truth often is.

Everyone who contributes to my well-being IS a part of me because I would not be me without them.

Let's take a personal inventory.

Who produced the food we ate today?

Who produced the clothes we wore today?

Who built the house or apartment we live in today?

Who made the bed we sleep on each night?

Who paved the roads we drive on each day on the way to work?

Who built the car we drive each day?

How many people had to do what they do well for us to have a good day?

I hope you get my point.

If you do all that on your own, take a bow.

If not, acknowledge that all those people who support us daily are very much a part of us that we do not yet know.

Next time you meet a "stranger,"...remember.

VOLUME 3

Mirror to the Way Forward

Knowing is not enough

Talk to the best and brightest people and ask them, "what are the keys to your success?" Invariably they'll say something most of us already know...hard work...diligent study...thinking outside the box...buying low, and selling high...

blah...Blah...BLAH!

We walk away, assuming they are being coy with their treasured secrets to success. The thing is...they actually are telling the truth. But you say, "If that's all it takes to be successful, I would be very successful. I already know all those keys to success." And now for our Yoda moment: It's not what you know. Instead, it IS what you DO that determines your success.

Consider investing. The first rule of investing is "buy low and sell high." Yet, when a scandal hits a company...the stock usually plummets. Why? Because an increasing number of investors are choosing to sell low. And when a company posts record profits...the stock price skyrockets. Why? Because an increasing number of investors are buying high. Now take Warren Buffett, one of America's greatest investors. On Black Monday, October 19, 1987, the stock market posted the deepest crash since the stock market crash of 1929. On this day, on paper, Warren Buffett lost over a billion dollars. And while the broad market was selling everything at increasingly lower prices, Warren Buffett bought the holdings that would drive his return on investment for the next decade and beyond. Everyone trading stock that day knew to buy low and sell high, but only a few actually did it. The key to Warren Buffett's investment success is he lives the maxim, even when the rest of the market is running in the other direction.

The simple lesson here is to make sure the best we know is reflected in the most we do.

Now ask yourself...Do I do unto others as I would have them do to me? Do I live the values I hope to receive from others? Do I give first what I want to receive? Am I the change that I expect in others? Do I listen with the same desire as I want to be heard?

Now imagine what life would be like if we did.

Dying from survival

You know what I mean. To spend each day doing whatever you must to keep the lights on...to make sure your family is provided for...to hold it all together for one more day. Dying from survival is allowing your soul to fade slowly away from lack of fulfillment...void of purpose...resigned to the task of pushing your bolder up that damn hill again and again.

To what end?

There is more to this life than stacking coins of security. Remember when you didn't even know about the grind? Yes, we were all young...dreaming about life before obligations. Actually feeling moments of happiness, unencumbered by responsibility.

That you still exist. This is who we are supposed to be. Our life is fulfilled by reaching toward our aspirations, unhindered by hunger or thirst or illness or lack of opportunity.

Our restoration resides beyond this paradigm we know all too well. The moment we stop living to make money is the instant we reclaim our true destiny...and recover the well-spring of our humanity.

We did not evolve to only survive.

The First Step toward the Future

There comes the point in every life when you first suspect something you always knew to be true may not be. For me, this moment was long in coming. Like the faintest whisper in a dark room, I have felt for some time my core American values that have defined my life were hollow and untrue. Yet it has only been in the last few years that I fully realized why.

To understand my journey, I must reveal a bit of my story. I was raised by an amazing woman who invested her time and resources into her two sons. Growing up in the Bronx (NY), she worked two jobs to send us to twelve years of the best Catholic education available in New York. We both graduated from the prestigious Cardinal Spellman High School (Justice Sotomayor graduated from Spellman in 1972). After high school, I served four years of active duty in the US Army. President Reagan was my Commander-in-Chief, and General Colin Powell was my V Corps commander while I served as a member of NATO in Germany.

After my enlistment, I attended college in Texas and graduate school in Connecticut before serving a one-year stint as a Lead Disaster Assistance Loan Officer in FEMA for the Northridge earthquake disaster. For the last 30 years, I have worked as a financial services professional, primarily as a small business banker.

During most of my youth, I was a registered democrat, changing in 1998 to a registered republican, only to change again to a registered independent by 2004. I had participated in one political campaign as a Surrogate Speaker for Matt Salmon (R) when he ran for Arizona Governor in 2002 (we lost to Janet Napolitano). I voted for Barack Obama in 2008 and 2012, and for the first time in my life, I voted for the Green Party candidate, Dr. Jill Stein, for President in 2016. By the 2020 general election, I voted for each political office except President. For most of my life, I have been a true patriot who believed in serving a cause bigger than myself. The virtues of independence, individual liberty, limited government, and the pursuit of happiness have defined my life.

Yet, in retrospect, I see the signs that led to my discontent starting in 1971 with the famous Powell memorandum...a call to arms for Corporate America to contribute a material portion of their earnings to the cause of transforming the government, academic scholarship, and the media to the advancement of corporate interests. By 1987, the glorification of corporate interest found popular expression in the motion picture *Wall Street*, where Gordon Gekko proudly proclaimed, "Greed is good."

Then in 1992, America elected a smooth-talking man of the people from Hope, Arkansas, who presented a new pro-business, socially liberal democrat. During Bill Clinton's tenure, he led Congress to ratify NAFTA, signed federal welfare reform, the 1994 crime bill, and as a parting gift repealed Glass-Steagall and deregulated complex financial instruments. Each of these measures proved to be devastating for poor, working, and middle-class Americans and enormously beneficial for corporate interests.

In November 2000, we elected an encore named George W. Bush, who fully monetized the military-industrial complex. President Bush codified the predicate for permanent war with the concepts of "pre-emptive war" and the "war on terror." Tax cuts in 2001 and 2003, coupled with the Medicare Part D bonanza for the pharmaceutical industry, produced an economy where business was booming through 2006. Wall Street's mortgage back security con, made legal by Bill Clinton in 1999, blew up the global residential real estate market by 2008. And to the rescue came Barack Obama, Nancy Pelosi, and congressional democrats who joined Bush in bailing out the corporate interests while millions of Americans lost their homes, jobs, and retirement savings.

Eight years of Obama, two with total democratic control, and all we have to show for it is this stupid tee-shirt saying, "Yes we can!" Little did I know the back of the shirt says, "I always draw the short straw no matter what major political party I support." As I said, "this moment of truth was long in coming." Now, where from here?

The American electorate has woken up. In 2016, republican primary voters rejected establishment republicans, and general election voters rejected the ultimate democratic establishment politician. Our national tragedy was not offering the American electorate a credible non-establishment option. Democratic Party shenanigans, exposed by WikiLeaks and others, prevented Senator Sanders from being the credible non-establishment option. Instead, America elected an owner of the establishment politicians the People had soundly rejected. Corporate interests were now the government.

The 2020 presidential election demonstrated the complete corporate capture of both major political parties by renominating President Trump and resurrecting President Obama's former Vice President Joe Biden.

Heads: the corporations win; Tails: everyone else loses.

The only question remaining is whether the deeply disgruntled, ethnically, regionally, faithfully, and racially divided American electorate will see past the divide and conquer strategy of corporate interest and finally identify the cause of our American nightmare. The moment we do, we will finally take our first step toward the future.

Fortunate One

President Kennedy was right. "Our problems are man-made. Therefore, they can be solved by man."

As we consider all the problems affecting our lives, let our consideration start with ourselves. What about our situation, our values, and our choices are contributing to the problems we see? For me, most of my choices have been consumed with providing for myself and my family. And as I look back over my life, I realize how much pride and satisfaction I experienced when I achieved success. Yet, with each success, I foreclosed the same opportunity for every person who didn't get hired or competed but failed to close the big deal. I'm familiar with their misery because I, too, have been defeated on many occasions.

My takeaway is something is deeply wrong with people having to compete to provide for themselves and their families. The competition is inherently unfair because our access to education and skill development is tied to the randomness of birth. None of us selects the families we are born into or the countries of our birth. Therefore, our success in the competition of life is more driven by luck than talent or hard work. My pride in providing for my family is a celebration of good fortune at the expense of others. As I am confronted by the problems resulting from accumulated misfortune, I must own my contribution and do something about it.

The first step of fundamental change is realizing where you stand is no longer acceptable. But what can be done?

Good fortune is a function of this life, no matter what we do. Some people are healthier, stronger, faster, possess a greater aptitude for learning, etc. For people who are fortunate, the opportunity to make great contributions to society is likely. But good fortune should not determine our ability to provide for ourselves and our families. There is no honor in denying the less fortunate the resources they need, especially when we possess the technology and resource capacity to sustainably provide for all of humanity.

Let Freedom Ring!

I am a free man.

Today, I awoke to a beautiful Saturday morning.

I am free to make this day all it can be; to get in my car and drive in any direction; to visit my family and friends; to strengthen my body with exercise and nutritious food.

In truth, I am free to go as far as my bank account and credit cards will allow me to go. My bills are paid, and I have a few hundred dollars left in my budget to spend before I get paid next Friday. But I won't get paid next Friday if I don't show up to work on Monday. Therefore, I am free from now through Sunday.

I am free to choose my vocation; if I accept, the compensation will set the boundaries of my freedom and the freedom of my family.

I am free to live anywhere I want—if I can pay the cost to live there.

If I get sick, I am free to see any doctor or seek any treatment I can afford to pay for.

In other words, I am a free[*] man.

And yet, I'm one of the lucky ones.

---

[*] subject to my capacity to earn money.

Lost

How did I get here? So far from my aspirations, I can no longer remember what they were.

I'm a banker.

I help business owners access the capital they need to develop and grow their businesses. I'm good at it. I actually enjoy adding value to my client's business operations. The thrill for me is that no request is the same. Each borrower is unique. I immerse myself into their life's story, and out of my review emerges a unique strategy to improve their business.

Why am I not fulfilled?

Money.

I help people by providing the optimal amount of money to achieve their financial goals. And while this is the best I can do given our free-market economy, I know the accumulation of money is the primary cause of the inequality that pervades modern life.

Despite the virtue of individual liberty, we are one humanity. We share one planet that produces a finite amount of resources at any given time. We ALL need money to access the resources that sustain us.

As I help my clients accumulate money, I must acknowledge the unintended consequence: resource deprivation for so many other people who don't have money.

Therefore, I am lost.

And I won't be found until I reconcile my vocation with my humanity.

The Wisdom of Parables

The thing about parables is the story does not have to be true for the lesson to be valid. We often use parables in the form of fairy tales, such as Disney movies, or even scriptural stories to teach children important lessons about life. Adults, too, can benefit from parables.

Consider the scriptural parable of the rich man and Lazarus. The story involves a beggar (Lazarus) living outside the front gate of a wealthy family's estate. Every day, the members of the family pass Lazarus as they enter the beautiful estate compound without giving Lazarus any consideration. Finally, the patriarch of the family dies and is condemned to eternal suffering. He is made to suffer as Lazarus suffered because he had every opportunity to relieve Lazarus's suffering and chose instead to offer him scorn and indifference. He is told that every member of his family who does nothing for Lazarus will suffer the same fate. Therefore, his suffering is deepened by the realization that his example will now condemn all his loved ones to eternal damnation.

What is the lesson of the rich man and Lazarus?

For years I thought the lesson was to do unto others as you would have them do to you. Most recently, I have come to understand that wealth in a finite, resourced world necessarily causes deprivation. To accumulate resources beyond our capacity to use denies resources to other people who desperately need them. Therefore, the morale of the story is not the rich man's lack of generosity; it is the rich man's gluttony that caused Lazarus's deprivation.

In America today, we are the rich man because our wealth is derived from our disproportionate, non-sustainable extraction of global resources for ourselves. And Lazarus is the billions of resource-deprived people who are slowly migrating to the front gate of the American estate.

Where once our front gate was opened wide:

"Give me your tired, your poor, Your huddled masses **yearning** to breathe free, The **wretched** refuse of your teeming shore, Send these, the **homeless, tempest-tost** to me, I lift my lamp beside the golden door!"[*]

Now we close the gate, build walls, and offer scorn to the refugees who only seek the promise of what America used to be.

---

[*] Public Domain Excerpt from "The New Colossus" written by Emma Lazarus and posted on a plaque on the base of the Statue of Liberty.

Change Happens When We Choose to Take the First Step

Contemplate the important factors that make your life meaningful...the person you share your life with...your children... your chosen vocation...a personal passion like painting or writing. For each of these factors, we made a simple choice that opened up the possibility for a lifetime of fulfilling experiences. At the moment of that first choice, we may have had no idea how impactful our decision would become. Yet as small, subtle, and seemingly insignificant as that first choice may have been at the time, our lives would be profoundly less satisfying had we made a different choice.

This is how change occurs.

As we consider our present state of personal fulfillment, we have the opportunity to make a choice to seek the fulfillment we deeply desire; or we can choose to do what we are already doing, which only resigns us to a life of fleeting moments of happiness. This commentary is written for everyone who chooses to seek fulfillment.

How do I get from where I am to a fulfilling life?

Assess where you are. How do you spend your days? What drives the decisions that frame your life? Given how you spend your time, how much of your day is spent doing things you would not do but for the need for money? Assess how money defines your relationships, activities, skills, interests, outlook, self-worth, security, health, wellness, stature, and worldview.

Does any of this serve you? Does any of this impact your personal fulfillment? Do you think more money would lead to your fulfillment? If not money, then what will it take?

The first step toward your fulfillment is realizing where you stand does not serve you.

Ok, if I am not fulfilled working hard every day, playing by the rules, paying my taxes, and doing everything society expects me to do, then what will it take?

We organize our lives based on a core set of social values taught to us by our families and reinforced by the cultural expressions of our society. As an American, these values are independence, self-interest, competition, and the pursuit of our own happiness. These values define our politics (democracy) and our economics (capitalism). These values emphasize individualism over community, encourage competition as a means of validating privilege, and accommodate dehumanizing deprivation as the price for losing.

In America, the poor do not hate the rich because they aspire to be rich one day. The rich do not lift the poor out of poverty because deprivation is the incentive for the poor to work themselves out of poverty. Both the rich and the poor share a common commitment to our core American values. Yet most people, regardless of their wealth, are not fulfilled.

Why?

There is an economic concept called the law of diminishing returns, which refers to the satisfaction we realize as we experience a phenomenon multiple times. For example, consider your satisfaction if you eat your favorite meal tonight. Then tomorrow, your best friend takes you out and pays for you to have your favorite meal again. Then your boss takes you to lunch to celebrate a promotion and again buys you your favorite meal. For most people, eating your favorite meal would be less enjoyable on the third day than it was the first day. The law of diminishing returns is a meaningful method for assessing the endurance of our personal satisfaction and a thoughtful means of distinguishing personal satisfaction from fulfillment.

Satisfaction brings us fleeting moments of happiness, but fulfillment brings us joy that never wanes. Consider how you feel when you do something that really makes a difference in the life of someone you love. Do you ever get bored with this feeling? This is fulfillment.

Now consider the experiences in your life that generate fulfillment. Do any of these experiences emphasize your individual interest over the interest of anyone else? In fact, if we are completely honest, the one common denominator of experiences that bring fulfillment is our commitment to any interest beyond our own.

By reconsidering the virtue of self-interest, we take the next critical step toward a life of fulfillment.

Death Demystified

We have been taught death is about loss.

We mourn death.

We cry, tear clothing...fall into despair.

No more hugs. No more long conversations into the early morning light.

They are gone.

Yet while they were here, did we see them every day? No.

And though we didn't always see them or talk to them, they enriched our lives every day.

How? Because our love made us one.

Regardless of what life offered, we knew how they thought and what they would say. We knew they loved and supported us come what may. Knowing them made our lives better.

Does death make us forget? No.

Losing physical contact is a profound loss, but once we make the emotional and spiritual connection through the love we share, we never, EVER lose each other.

Therefore, we should love as many people as we can. Certainly, every person who contributes to making our lives worth living because in the absence of genuine love, physical connection is all we share...

...And death truly becomes a total loss.

The Dilemma of Money

Beyond the root of all evil, money is...

A lifeline to the resources that sustain us.

Often the difference between life and death.

The overseer on the modern plantation.

The sufficient condition for social interaction.

The great un-equalizer.

The Midas Touch of human relationships.

Our addictive undoing.

The culmination of the old paradigm.

The limit of our humanity.

The lowest denominator of infinity.

The zero-sum of our abundance.

The price of our dignity.

The excuse for our disillusionment.

Our unfixable fix.

A stairway to nowhere...

The crass reduction of purpose into objectification.

The value of scarcity.

The sign of the times.

The incentive for our extinction.

And yet the reality of our condition is we must seek money to survive another day.

By acknowledging the gilded shackles that bind us, we illuminate the path to our fulfillment.

Who Am I?

For almost all my life, I thought I was what society taught me to be...

A man, brother, son, father, husband, friend, banker, American... a human.

Then a new realization entered my consciousness: I am not my perception.

Before I could come to this new revelation, I had to set aside the cultural virtue distilled by Descartes: "Cogito Ergo Sum" [translated "I think, therefore I am"].

My discovery is not unique. It is one among an emerging understanding expressed by diverse sources that reflect the dawning of a new paradigm.

I cannot *be* my perception because I create my perception. My perception changes as I experience life. As I learn the lessons of my experience, my perception becomes a more accurate expression of how life works. Ultimately, the wisdom of my perception combined with our cultural expectations led me to assume my perception of myself...is myself. It is not.

If I am not my perception, who am I?

I am energy.

I am currently embodied in human form to experience the limitations that only life can provide.

I surge when I grow close to other energy sources and ebb when I am isolated.

My energy transfers and even accelerates when I give or receive love. And then, I am no longer limited to my own body.

I am part of something that exceeds this isolated, individualistic assumption of our existence.

I become Us.

Who are you?

Aphorisms for the soul

Freedom is a mirage that encourages us to act without consideration of the impact on others.

Earn is a euphemism for entitlement to resources regardless of need.

Self-interest is a rationalization that accommodates casual cruelty.

American exceptionalism is hubris masking global exploitation.

They hate us because we gorge ourselves on their resources and expect them to like it.

The human body is not self-sustaining because it produces few of the things it needs for survival.

Scarcity is a discretionary trait of an immature society.

Gluttony is claiming resources beyond your capacity to use.

Interdependence is life because it describes how we exist.

Independence is death because we can't exist free from air, water, food, humanity, nature...

Automation and artificial intelligence are threats to our wellbeing, only if earning money through a job remains a prerequisite for acquiring the resources we need to survive.

Living daily with one foot on a banana peel

Here we are, working harder—and hopefully smarter—toward the common goal of financial independence. To reach a point where we can choose to spend our limited time as we see fit. Yet, no matter how close we are to achieving our goal, we all live one mishap away from carrying a "work for food" sign at the side of the road.

How? Reliance on money.

If you have it, your possibilities appear endless. And if you don't, you may starve to death while living in the wealthiest country in recorded history.

Consider one startling fact: Almost all of us have lost loved ones to curable, preventable diseases because they did not possess enough money to gain the knowledge of healthy nutrition, or to purchase food that supports wellness, or to access timely and adequate medical treatment.

Have you noticed that the highest quality goods and services are reserved only for people who have the money to pay the most? For the rest of us, we are immersed in an ocean of sub-optimal products and services that are designed to rapidly degrade, so we will have little choice but to purchase the products again and again. And the worst part is many of us suffer injuries and even death resulting from the less than optimal quality of the goods and services we rely on.

This is the unspoken reality of our lives.

Up until this moment, we have been told price discrimination in the quality of goods and services is necessary because there are simply not enough resources to provide the best for everyone. The accumulation of human knowledge, coupled with relentless technological developments, has rendered scarcity of the highest quality goods and services obsolete. Stated bluntly, we now have the capability to provide the best quality for all of us.

I hear your doubt but consider a few easily verifiable facts...

- Knowledge, once gained, can benefit everyone. The only reason knowledge is withheld is to give contributors exclusive rights that are sold to make money.

- Most of the garbage gorging our global landfills is from affordable (cheap) goods that were produced to fail long before the best quality goods.

- Most of the drain on global resources is for the production of less than optimal quality goods that are sold at prices that support our consumption-based economy. As every economist insists, the more we consume, the better the economy. Better for whom?

- Since the best quality is reserved only for people who can afford to pay the most, the large majority of global millionaires make their fortunes selling sub-optimal products and services to the rest of us.

- Our current mass production of sub-optimal goods and services threatens to exhaust global resources as billions of new customers join the consumption pool, especially in India and China.

And what are the implications? If we fail to improve the efficiency of global resource utilization, future resource availability will support materially smaller global populations.

What can be done?

Educate yourself on the issue of scarcity. If we have the technology and resources to provide the highest quality goods and services to everyone, price discrimination is no longer necessary.

The Price of Winning...

The thing about success today is it is all about winning.

Getting the big promotion. Being hired for the great job. Signing the big client. Having your dream woman or man say, "yes I will marry you." Writing the latest *New York Times* #1 best seller. Buying the winning Powerball ticket. Supporting the Super Bowl champion team...

Yet the cost of winning is producing far more losers.

Have you given much consideration to what happens to the losers? This is a trick question because all of us know exactly what happens to the losers, since we have all lost many times. When we don't get the big promotion or get hired for the dream job or our perfect man or woman says "no," the whole trajectory of our lives changes. The range of choices we have to provide for ourselves and our families is diminished. And as these losses pile up, we find ourselves acquiescing to lives of faded dreams.

But the cost of losing is not just aspirational.

The quality of the food we eat, the comfort of our shelter, the security of our neighborhood, our access to timely & effective healthcare, and so much more are all tied to our wins and losses.

For those of us who have more wins than losses, we are encouraged to feel we earned the spoils of our victories. And for the rest of us, we are encouraged to accept lives made excessively harder and often shorter as the cost of losing.

It is nothing short of casual cruelty to know we waste more than enough resources to provide nutritious food, safe housing, and quality healthcare for the less fortunate among us.

The fact that we don't, reveals the true price of winning... the loss of our basic humanity.

I really want to know...

...Who are you?

Not the choices you make or the thoughts you have, or the concepts and symbols you identify with. None of these options are you.

Why is knowing you important?

Because once you know who *you* are, you can see who *we* are. And thereafter, you will see truth unfiltered by the layers of your preferences.

Do you know who you are? Time to find out.

We Learn to Live by How We Play

Who are your teams?

Mine were the Yankees, Cowboys, Celtics, and the Islanders. Hmm, I can feel your judgment.

Even if you hate sports, you still have teams.

Ford or Chevy or Toyota...

Verizon or AT&T or Sprint or T-Mobile...

And now that we are adults, our teams play for keeps.

Democrat or Republican or MAGA...

Conservative or Liberal or Moderate...

Man or Woman...American or not American...

Us versus Them.

In our games, winners take all the glory...and the losers are resigned to the scrap heap of history.

In real life, the winners earn more than they can ever use...and the losers wind up carrying a sign on the offramp of life, marginalized and forgotten.

Yet have you ever really thought about what separates the winners from the losers?

Once you think past the ego-based answers: talent, intelligence, willingness to work hard...You start to realize how things well beyond your control are more important: the family & country of your birth, who you know, being in the right place at the right time, random luck, etc.

So, as we sip our high-quality beverage of choice, consider how easily our good fortune could have been different. And if it was different, how comfortable we are enjoying our good fortune without a thought about the people who weren't as lucky.

Yes, we learn to live by the games we play. Yet aren't we all more than these uniforms we wear? Are any of our successes really by our efforts alone? Do we have no experiences where our personal satisfaction does not come at someone else's expense?

Winning is a hollow victory based on a false choice: win or lose.

Life offers a third option...fulfillment, which is only possible when no one loses.

Expectations...our self-imposed Truman Show

Newborn babies are innocent because they have undeveloped expectations. New experiences are an unfiltered phenomenon. But with each experience, the infant's mind records the responses and feelings and begins the lifelong development of situational expectations. The baby quickly learns who feeds them, who cleans them, and who takes care of them. And when the baby needs something, the baby will communicate their newly learned expectation to the parents who take care of them.

This process of expectation development serves us our entire lives. As our experiences and education accumulate, we develop comprehensive expectations of everything affecting our lives. Our sense of personal satisfaction became a function of how our experiences match our expectations. And this is where our disillusionment comes from.

Consider the following thought experiment:

Set aside your expectations—and experience each moment as it actually happens.

The more we experience life as it occurs, the more we learn how wrong our expectations can be. Why?

Nothing around us ever remains the same. As the hour hand on a clock, everything we experience is in a constant state of change. Yet we will never notice if we see life through the prism of our expectations.

Ever wonder how a California Dime became the Ol' Ball & Chain?

Simply look at her as if she is the same woman you have seen a thousand times before.

Turn off your self-imposed Truman Show and discover how vivid life can be.

Breadcrumbs

Truth is the pattern of how things work.

What is true has always been true.

There is truth and everything else that is not true. The difference is only truth is eternal.

Truth is realized through our understanding, but our understanding is not limited to the truth. As such, the truth can only be found inside you.

Consider your opinion, which changes as you learn new information. The quality of your opinion is a function of its proximity to truth. Once you learn the truth, your opinion evolves into knowledge.

Knowledge is power because it serves as a breadcrumb to remind you who you are.

Wisdom occurs once you remember.

VOLUME 4

Out of the Ashes of a Pandemic

The Day after the Financial Crash

We have been there before. October 30, 1929...October 20, 1987...September 30, 2008. On these days, we had as much food on the shelves of our stores as we did the day before. We had as many suitable homes capable of sheltering us from harsh weather. We still had jobs and meaningful work to do. What changed?

The financial markets were desperately short of money. The availability and quality of resources that made our lives worth living had been unaffected. But the severe shortage of cash led over time to the devastating waste of enormous resources destroyed by neglect. Crops shriveled in the fields, the assembly line stopped producing products, homes were abandoned, jobs were lost, savings were lost, marriages were destroyed, and broad access to higher education was eliminated. All because money was in too few hands.

Money has become a surrogate for resources. If you have money, you can access resources. And if you lose your money, your access to resources is taken away. The thing is...money is not resources. Money is a totally arbitrary way to determine access to resources. Would any of us have the money and, therefore, the access to resources we have if we were born to the lowest caste in India? Or to an impoverished single mother in rural Appalachia? Yet we compound the randomness of birth with the use of money as a surrogate for resources to determine who is able to reach their full potential.

Given this reality, who among the fortunate can honestly claim they earned the privilege they enjoy at the expense of the less fortunate? In the parable of Lazarus and the rich man, we are all the rich man. According to the Worldwatch Institute, 12 percent of the world's population living in North America and Western Europe accounts for 60 percent of private consumption spending, while the one-third living in South Asia and sub-Saharan Africa account for only 3.2 percent. Our disproportionate consumption of global resources creates the conditions for mass deprivation of billions of people, few of which have the opportunity to reach their full potential.

The system of global economics that produces these inhumane conditions is not sustainable. We are experiencing resource depletion, destabilization of political institutions, a global refugee crisis involving mass migration to more fortunate countries, radicalized populations fueling global terrorism, and the exploding addictions to drugs and alcohol as more and more people self-medicate to cope with the inadequacy of available choices to improve their lives.

Our choice is becoming clear: change to a full access, sustainable, resource management based, global economy, or degrade into a modern dystopia where fewer resources are available to sustain fewer people.

They are Our Enemy

They who divide us.

They who benefit from our fighting.

They who win while the rest of us lose.

They who own our government.

They who control the resources that sustain us.

They are the cause of our American nightmare.

Who are They? The nameless, faceless, thoughtless They?

They are the hoarders who derive their gluttonous wealth from the productivity of our labor.

Yet, They are the embodiment of the values we are taught to live by.

Nonetheless, They are getting worried.

They realize we are awakening. Too many of us see past their grand illusion.

Try as They may, They can't conceal the Big Lie behind the prevailing narrative they sell.

We are beginning to see who They are...where They are...and how They control us.

They have privilege, but the power is provided by our consent.

Now ask yourself: who stands in the way of your highest aspirations?

They who claim everything.

They are our enemy.

There is Enough for All of Us

Free-market economics is considered the most efficient (fair) way to distribute scarce goods and services. But what if human innovation, technological development, and available natural resources have rendered scarcity unnecessary?

What if it is not necessary to compete to eat...learn... have shelter...receive the care we need... reach our full potential... be contributing members of a global community? Would you still prefer to pursue your own happiness at the expense of others?

Doubtful.

Technological developments are rapidly eliminating the jobs many people rely on to support themselves and their families. Sadly, many people view this fact as the tragic cost of modernity. But what if automation and AI are paving the way for humanity to free ourselves from the need to have a job to support our well-being?

We would be free to cultivate and apply the boundless, creative capabilities of human ingenuity to the areas of science, mathematics, the arts, philosophy, and so much more. Free to invest in every person so each of us can reach our full potential in the areas of our vocational passion, unconstrained by financial discrimination.

This is not utopian mythology.

This is a reality once we each accept that the scarcity of the goods and services that support our well-being is no longer necessary.

If there really is enough for all of us, we no longer need to take as much for ourselves as possible.

The fact is free-market economic principles of advancing our own self-interest encourage us to take all we can, which creates the scarcity causing global human suffering.

Be the change. Life can be a global feast. Have some and pass it on.

Why Capitalism is Failing

Capitalism was made possible by the emergence of democratic societies. These societies shed economic elitism and allowed increasing portions of the population to access wealth.

The core engine of capitalism is one of the most common instincts...greed. Hard work, skill acquisition, and innovation can combine to elevate a child born in poverty to great wealth and prosperity. Under these circumstances, everyone has a chance to earn financial independence. And as a result, there is no need for the poor to resent the rich because they too have the opportunity to be rich one day.

What went wrong? Greed

As the descendants of poverty elevated to great wealth, their greed inspired them to use their resources to manipulate the free market to consolidate wealth for themselves at the expense of everyone else.

The propensity of free-market capitalism to create severe wealth inequality is not new. Historically, these periods of severe financial imbalance were corrected by economic depressions, which re-leveled the opportunity to access wealth for the broader society.

By the 1970s, the Powell memorandum encouraged wealthy people to protect their interests by investing enormous resources to co-opt the government, university system, and mass media. The point of these investments was to prevent economic correction that restores financial opportunities for the general population.

In the 1990s, Alan Greenspan accomplished the first "soft" landing in US history by reversing a business cycle slow down without an economic recession. And by 2009, Congress and the Federal Reserve prevented the new Great Depression by giving the wealthiest holders of capital trillions of dollars in public funds to cover private losses. The net effect is to metastasize severe economic inequality as the new norm of the free-market economy.

Free-market manipulation and economic globalism, combined with accelerated automation, have effectively subjugated the broad working class to involuntary servitude.

While the wealthy have been successfully preventing the restoration of economic opportunity for the general population, they have also earned the contempt of people who now understand they will never have financial security.

Our time has arrived

We are living at a transformative moment in history. As free-market economics and liberal democracy crumble, we will all have an opportunity to participate in how to rebuild society and the economy.

The one advantage of suffering through our failing economics and political system is being inspired by the necessity to innovate the next stage of our social evolution. For many people, this reality may sound frightening, but consider how we were living was not sustainable for the country or the world.

The cost of what was normal life included a perpetual growth economic system that has destabilized the ecology that sustains humanity. The extraordinary accumulation of greenhouse gas emissions from the utilization of fossil fuels is warming the planet to dangerous levels that threaten to decimate the biodiversity necessary for human life.

As such, normal life was going to change.

Thankfully, we now have a unique opportunity to reconsider how we use global resources in order to establish a new life that aligns with our natural environment.

We each have a role to play in the formation of the next economy and society.

Please appreciate the fact that people will be making these decisions whether we participate or not.

My hope is each of us will give serious thought to how we can all contribute to this rare opportunity to develop a sustainable society for ourselves and our progeny.

The Evil in My Mirror

When I consider how a person can join with strangers to study scripture, then stand up and murder nine worshippers, including the pastor...I recoil in the face of evil.

When I turn on the news to learn a young man used an assault rifle to slaughter twenty 5-year-old children...I recoil in the face of evil.

When I live in a pristine community where an assassin enters a supermarket on a beautiful Saturday morning and shoots a congresswoman in the head, then turns his weapon on random strangers, killing an eight-year-old girl, a federal district judge, and eight people in total until he is subdued while reloading his assault rifle...I recoil in the face of evil.

When an independently wealthy man uses a sniper's rifle from his carefully chosen hotel room to kill random strangers at an outdoor music concert...I recoil in the face of evil.

And yet, as distraught as I am, I am left wondering what about American society produces so many heinous incidents?

One thing connecting these incidents is the emotional detachment each killer feels for the victims. In the absence of clinical mental illness, what explains dehumanizing emotional detachment?

Competition.

Competition is one of the most important American virtues, so much so that we celebrate and even glorify success born out of competition, while we feel nothing for the losers.

We compete in the games we play. We compete for the friends we have. We compete for lovers, spouses, and possessions. We compete for every grade in school, every honor we achieve, and every dollar we obtain.

When we consider how we take care of ourselves and our families, we accept as a given the primary thing standing in the way of everything we want is other people doing all they can to get it too.

As I think of every job I have held, I can vividly remember the satisfaction I felt when I was offered the position. Missing from my memory was any thought of what happened to the people who didn't get the job. It wasn't that I didn't know what it felt like to not get the job. I have been there many times, and it can be dreadful, especially when bills are due. I just never gave those other people any consideration.

This detachment is how we dehumanize each other.

This is how we sleep comfortably in our homes while countless people live and die on the streets. This is how hundreds of thousands of people die annually from preventable diseases in the wealthiest country on earth. This is how to serve and to protect...becomes an 8-minute and 46-second snuff film.

No more.

How can I extinguish the evil in my mirror?

By revealing my humanity...as I see yours.

Famous last words from both of our political parties

"As President and Commander-in-Chief, it is my duty to the American people to report that renewed hostile actions against United States ships on the high seas in the Gulf of Tonkin have today required me to order the military forces of the United States to take action in reply." [President Lyndon B. Johnson]

"You must pursue this investigation of Watergate even if it leads to the President. I'm innocent. You've got to believe I'm innocent." [President Richard Nixon]

"I, Gerald R. Ford, President of the United States...do grant a full, free, and absolute pardon unto Richard Nixon."

"Explanation we received why the first action of the new Iranian government was to attack the US embassy and take American hostages. [Absent quote from President Jimmy Carter]

"There he goes again." [President Ronald Reagan – 1980 and 1984]

"Read my lips, no new taxes." [President George H.W. Bush]

"I did not have sexual relations with that woman." [President Bill Clinton]

"Explanation we received for why we were attacked on 9/11 [Absent quote from President George W. Bush]

"Change will not come if we wait for some other person or some other time. We are the ones we've been waiting for. We are the change that we seek." [President Barack Obama]

"We will make America strong again. We will make America safe again. And we will make America great again, greater than ever before." [President Donald Trump]

Now our choice as President is the architect of mass incarceration who is being portrayed as the virtuous alternative to the past cretin in chief.

Does anyone notice the tragic analogy to the George Floyd murder?

For at least the last fifty years, our political parties have held their knee on the neck of the American people.

Today, "MAGA" deplorables are suffering as much as the "Libtards." And while we hate each other, the government sworn to protect us is squeezing the air out of our lungs.

Now is the time to set aside the labels and form a new political party for the people, by the people, and comprised of the people.

The Right Lesson from History

For many people, modernity is like listening to an old 45 album at 78 speed. Too much, too fast to figure anything out. People just drown out the white noise by focusing their energies on the day-to-day realities of their lives. Unfortunately, like the frog in the slowly warming water, most people are realizing the white noise is smothering their day-to-day existence.

Now what?

Fear has led us to grasp onto easy answers con artists who give us the tools and scapegoats to express our anger and frustration.

How has all the ranting served us?

Welcome to the Divided States of America.

If there is any good news here, it is the system is imploding. All the speed bumps that historically saved our society from overheating have been co-opted by the ruling elite. We have reached the logical extreme of the American experiment. And like with all logical extremes, the theory is not performing as intended.

COVID-19 was nature's Trojan Horse. Healthier societies were able to limit the damage. Toxic societies have been consumed by it. What emerges in the post-pandemic era will offer the hope of a new global power structure.

Could it be more equitable than the last?

Only if humanity has finally learned the right lesson from history.

Like the Air We Breathe

Compassion is the natural emotional response to all that gives us life.

Consider what gives you life?

None of us produce clean air, but we all pollute it with each exhale of carbon dioxide. One critical function of the billions of trees on earth is to clean the air of carbon. Accordingly, trees give us life.

Nutrient-rich foods give us life because this is how we obtain critical vitamins and minerals not produced by our bodies. Nutritious food requires nutrient-rich soil, which is comprised of trillions of decomposed creatures accumulated over millions of years. Maintaining nutrient-rich soil requires the accumulation of knowledge built over thousands of years. Accordingly, many generations of people we will never know give us life.

Our bodies use pressure to circulate blood, oxygen, and essential nutrients. While our skin is designed to offer the first line of defense against infection, our skin is incapable of containing the inner pressure of our circulatory system without the assistance of the earth's atmospheric pressure. In deep space, our bodies would expand to twice the normal size as the vacuum of space would pull the air from our bodies, rupturing our lungs and killing us in the process. Accordingly, the earth's atmosphere gives us life.

I could go on, but I know you get the point.

The disconnect with most people in our society today is the idea that compassion is discretionary.

Compassion is the authentic response of any person who realizes their existence is interdependent on humanity and the ecology that sustains us.

Advancing our self-interest at the expense of the hands that sustain us is not only self-defeating but also pathologically detached from the reality of our daily lives.

Like the air we breathe, compassion is the essential emotion expressing appreciation for our existence.

Remember

Often in life, we do not realize what we cherish until we have lost it.

Occasionally, we are afforded a glimpse of what life would be like without our cherished desire, and the experience serves as a vivid reminder we can never forget.

2020 is our vivid reminder of our need for human touch.

Remember...

Seeing the smile of a stranger you held the door for...

Feeling a firm handshake of a new acquaintance...

Receiving a hug from a friend simply because you needed one...

Immersing in the exhilaration of the crowd at a great music concert...

Shimmying up to the bar to order drinks during happy hour...

Participating in the wave at your favorite sporting event...

Squeezing into a fully occupied elevator and feeling relieved because you made it in time...

This used to be our normal lives.

Life without human touch is sterile, virtual, and isolated.

Our communication lacks depth because, like texting, it is uninformed by body language or energetic vibration.

We are reduced to digital simulations that can more easily be labeled and categorized.

Consideration becomes quaint.

Cancel culture is rampant.

Mutual understanding is obsolete.

This is the new normal of a detached society.

Never forget how we felt in isolation.

As we move past COVID-19. The health implications of social interaction will restore to normal.

We will have the opportunity to reconnect with each other.

How we connect will be a function of the perspective we have gained.

We are one humanity.

Interdependently nourished by the natural environment that sustains us.

Remember...

2021 – The Year of the Economy

Recently I read a book written by an economist, Stephanie Kelton, called *The Deficit Myth*, which provided a comprehensive analysis of modern monetary theory (MMT). In essence, deficits do not matter because, as a sovereign fiat currency nation whose debt is entirely in our own currency, the United States can spend as much money as we need, with inflation being our only limiting factor. While I concur with the validity of MMT, I differ with Stephanie's claim that politicians in both political parties are not already thoroughly versed in MMT. They are. And the implications are profound.

The most cursory review of historical economic data shows two generations of politicians have purposely driven federal debt from $1 trillion dollars in 1980 to over $27 trillion dollars as of 2021 through the use of MMT.

Deficit spending paid for trillions of dollars of military spending, regressive tax cuts, a new entitlement (Medicare Part D) converted into a multi-trillion dollar boondoggle for the pharmaceutical industry, and a deregulation scheme that gutted environmental protection laws and repealed Glass-Steagall (to whom we have Bill Clinton to thank!) And pursuant to MMT, the trillions of dollars in annual deficits funneled surpluses to the private sector.

Tragically, a fiscal policy supported by both political parties targeted the trillions in surpluses to the wealthiest Americans that allowed American multinational corporations to off-shore labor, assets, and profits, further avoiding US taxation.

The GINI coefficient is the economic data point used to measure income and wealth inequality. A GINI coefficient of zero equals perfect economic equality, and one equals absolute economic inequality. According to the World Bank, the 1979 GINI coefficient in the US was .345 versus 2019 of .48 (source: Statista), a profound statistical indication of the increasing severity of income and wealth inequality in America. 2019 US GINI coefficient is tied for the 20th most unequal economy in the world with Costa Rica and by far the most unequal of all G7 nations (the UK is number 2 with .392). Yet this was all before COVID-19.

Since COVID-19 was declared a global pandemic, the US Congress had approved multiple stimulus packages by the end of 2020, with the most significant being the CARES Act approved in March 2020 and the recent $900 billion dollar stimulus package. The CARES Act, on its face, included $2.2 trillion dollars in economic stimulus, but also authorized the Federal Reserve to invest ten times the $425 billion dollar allocation for corporations with more than 500 employees (or $4.25 trillion dollars). A rough estimate of the distribution of the two stimulus packages follows:

Small Businesses (less than 500 employees) and
    Individuals =
$320B ($1,200 one-time payments)
$160B ($600 one-time payments)
$300B ($600/week Pandemic Unemployment Assistance
    or PUA)
$63B ($300/week PUA)

$480B (80% Payroll Protection Program or PPP; 20%
    poached by large corporations)
$285B (PPP 2nd round)
$25B (Rent support)
$10B (Childcare)
$1.643T
(25.2% of the two primary stimulus packages)

Large Corporations (500+ employees)
$75B (Airlines)
$425B (large company with 500+ employees)
$4,250B (Fed Reserve Investment)
$120B (PPP poaching)
$15B (Airline 2nd stimulus)
$4.885 trillion dollars
(74.8% of the two primary stimulus packages)
$6.528 trillion dollars[*]

By the end of 2020, the economic damage of COVID-19 included a 31% contraction in 2Q20 GDP (vs. 1Q20), 33% growth in 3Q20 GDP (vs. 2Q20 or 90% annualized of 2019 GDP), small businesses in operation down 29% since January 2020, net job loss of approximately ten million jobs (primarily for jobs with annual salaries of $27k/year or less where employment is down 20%, jobs with annual salaries over $60k/year have returned to pre-COVID-19 employment levels). 4Q20 data, including the critical holiday shopping season (Fed Chair stated retail sales are sluggish), had not yet been reported.

---

[*] (Total allocated excludes approximately $822 billion dollars, largely for emergency services, state & local government support, vaccination purchases & distribution, and a laundry list of heinous pork).

Given the fiscal stimulus has been heavily skewed toward large corporations versus small businesses or individuals (75% vs. 25%), Wall Street posted historic gains in 2020 versus 2019 despite the global pandemic:

Dow Industrials up 7.2%
S&P 500 up 16.3%
Russell 2000 up 18.4%
NASDAQ composite up 43.6% (highest since 2009)
Source: Wall Street Journal

As of 11/30/2020, US Billionaires' net worth increased one trillion dollars since the pandemic began (source: Statista and Americans for Tax Fairness).

According to the US Census Household Pulse Survey completed 12/21/2020:
33% of US households are having a hard time covering basic expenses.
33% expect joblessness to lead to eviction in the next 60 days.
12% report food shortages in their households.

Accordingly, COVID-19 has provided our political leaders the opportunity to use over $9 trillion dollars[†] in deficit spending and stimulus to exacerbate income and wealth inequality in America.

This is the US pandemic economy.

The American people cannot rely on the current political parties or politicians or establishment political or economic commentators for constructive support in rebuilding the post-

---

[†] ($9T = $5T in deficits (2020: $3.7T; 2021 so far: $1.329T [source: Congressional Budget Office] + $4.25T from the Federal Reserve)

pandemic economy.

As we entered 2021 (according to *Reuters*), Paul Krugman announced he expects the US economic recovery from the pandemic to be "much faster and continue much longer than many people expect." The Nobel Laureate in Economics cited higher US savings rates and pent-up demand as the drivers of the US economic recovery. Undoubtedly, the extraordinary savings and pent-up demand must be from the 60 percent of American households (excluding 29% small business failures) that are not living paycheck to paycheck and can afford a $400 unexpected expense. Tragically, 40 percent of US households do not qualify (according to Federal Reserve data & a Harvard University study).

Solutions to the economic challenges facing people impacted by the global pandemic will not be coming from establishment sources.

Therefore, I strongly recommend focusing our attention regarding the post-pandemic economy on non-establishment commentators such as Richard Wolff, Yanis Varoufakis, Peter Joseph, Chris Hedges, and Yuval Noah Harari.

Yuval Harari has written extensively about the economic impact of technological disruption, which has been accelerated by COVID-19. Take note of the extraordinary performance of the tech companies on the NASDAQ composite (up 43.6% vs. 2019). Large industrial corporations like General Motors (beyond buying back their own shares) are investing in automated technology to dramatically reduce the cost structure of their business models in anticipation of materially lower aggregate demand in the near term (3 to 5 years). Accelerating automation will make large portions of the working class "economically irrelevant" (according to Yuval Harari).

This is the discussion we need to have regarding the new post-pandemic economy.

Ecological sustainability is the reason why we must not simply restore the pre-COVID economy. While climate science and global environmental events are irrefutable, powerful fossil fuel interests continue to block meaningful progress to keep global average temperature increases from exceeding the critical limit of 1.5 degrees.

The prospect of a sixth mass extinction event has been warned by diverse commentators, including Pope Francis (see his 2015 encyclical *Laudato Si*) and David Attenborough (see his latest documentary released in September 2020: *A Life on Our Planet*).

The time is urgently now to escape the binary mythology of capitalism (developed in the 1700s) or socialism (developed in the 1800s) and innovate an economy of the 21st century. Much work has been done in this area.

Peter Joseph founded the Zeitgeist Movement (see https://www.thezeitgeistmovement.com/about/) in 2008 as a science-based economic sustainability project which advocates for a global resource management economic system informed by open source innovation and utilizing decentralized production. Peter is a deeply thoughtful, exceptionally articulate advocate for a new, redefined economy that aligns with equality and ecological sustainability. Peter's latest book, *The New Human Rights Movement*, was made into his latest film, "InterReflections," which was released in October 2020.

If 2020 was the year of COVID-19 exposed the failure of the old economy, 2021 would be the year where the green shoots of the Sustainable Economy emerge.

The Life We Seek

When you strip away all the labels and quiet the noise of our toxic society, you create space to remember who we are and how we survive each day.

We have food to eat because many people we will never know produced it and brought it to market so we can buy it.

We have shelter today because many people designed it, constructed it, and maintained it so we can buy or lease it.

We have clothes to wear...You get my point.

If you are grateful to be alive and appreciate the lifestyle you enjoy, steep on the fact that none of it is possible if you had to rely only on what your family and friends and people just like you produce.

If you find yourself fearing, hating, or hurting people who appear different from you, take this moment to acknowledge you are harming the hands that support you.

For those of us who have pets, we realize our pets bless us with unconditional love. Ever wonder why? They know very clearly who takes care of them every day.

Nothing in nature lives independently.

If you really want to change this toxic society, start by loving unconditionally the hands that feed you, clothe you, and produce everything you need that you are unable to produce for yourself.

The life we seek begins the moment we remember.

Thoughtlessness...
Our Persistent Pandemic

How do we get to a place where we fear/hate/harm the hands that serve us?

Democrats hating Republicans...

MAGA hating the establishment political parties...

Rural People hating City Slickers...

Wall Street hating Main Street...

Rich hating Poor...

Capitalists hating Environmentalists...

Us hating Them...

Everyone hating Anyone who hates them first...

Thoughtlessness.

How do we come to accept popular virtues as truth when they are disproved by our actual experience?

Independence...None of us live independently.

Freedom...Financial freedom only buys what other people produce.

Competition...When our bodies produce cells that compete, we call it cancer. As such, humanity is growing cancer in the ecology that sustains us.

Self-interest...produced the richest family in America, which employs hundreds of thousands of people that qualify for food stamps.

Thoughtlessness.

When we consider America's response to the COVID-19 pandemic...

We exercised our freedom to wear a mask or not,

We asserted our independence by socially distancing or not,

We demonstrated our insatiable competitive spirit by reopening local economies far too early,

We revealed the dominant self-interest by directing trillions of dollars to Wall Street while a third of all small businesses failed, working-class employment plummeted by 20 percent, and 12 percent of American households reported food shortages.

And the culmination is over a million pandemic-related deaths and counting, two-thirds of which could have been prevented.

Thoughtlessness.

Can we find our way out of the swamp of thoughtlessness? Absolutely.

Our persistent thoughtlessness pandemic will end the moment a critical mass of us remember who we are...

One human family, interdependently reliant on each other and the natural environment that sustains us.

The Elephant in the Room

We are all victims of cognitive dissonance, inspired by a society based on lies that our souls know aren't true. Time to call a spade a spade so we can all find peace.

We are not free. If we were, we would spend our time doing what brings us joy.

We are not independent. If we were, we would produce our own air, water, food, shelter, atmospheric pressure, biodiversity, language, and everything else we need to survive.

Competition is toxic when you must compete to eat. Currently, 12 percent of American households report food shortages. COVID-19 revealed in the competition for resources to take care of ourselves and our families, we are defeating the essential workers of our society...who are among the lowest earners in America.

Self-Interest is self-defeating. How long would any of us survive relying only on what our family and friends produce?

Humanity grew to dominate our planet by working symbiotically against our predators. And now that our predators are defeated, we are defeating each other and the natural ecology that sustains us.

To wake up from the nightmare we are living, all we need to do is remember who we are and how we survive each day.

Nothing to Fear

Are you sovereign?

You appear free, unencumbered by physical constraints, and in possession of the ability to make choices.

Yet look where we are...

Isolated, socially distant, living virtually, hiding behind masks, fearful of strangers...finding security in the magic injections provided by multi-national pharmaceutical companies who demonstrate they are more concerned about profits than saving as many lives as possible.

Are you safe now? Just long enough to buy the next booster shot. More magic from the Wizard.

How did we get so weak?

COVID-19 is more than a virus...it is a metaphor for all the reasons we are encouraged to give away our sovereignty.

Life is filled with many possibilities, some good and some bad. What actually happens in our lives is a function of choices we control and choices beyond our control. When a challenge like COVID-19 appears in our lives, we can choose to put our focus on the choices we can control or defer to choices outside our control.

We can make a choice to support our immune system. COVID-19 preys on compromised immune systems. For healthy, fully supported immune systems, COVID-19 is less dangerous than driving your car.

Or we can succumb to the fear that we are unable to protect ourselves without the paid assistance of a for-profit manufacturer who denies the magic injection to billions of people unable to pay their ransom.

What could go wrong?

For those of us with compromised immune systems, take a look at your medicine cabinet. Notice how what ails you never gets cured? Medication is designed to maintain you in relative "comfort" for as long as you keep taking it...forever. Will you ever get tired of being someone's revenue stream?

This is what happens when you give your sovereignty away.

Yet you still have a choice.

Our bodies are designed to heal. Find out what your body needs to produce wellness and do that.

The moment we reclaim our sovereignty, we will realize we have nothing to fear.

The Urgency of Now

As Americans, the virtues we are encouraged to use as guideposts for success impede our personal fulfillment because they are at odds with how we exist each day.

Nothing in nature lives independently. By design, we all are interdependent on each other and the natural environment that provides for us.

When the cells in our body compete, we call the condition cancer. Humanity is functioning like cancer to the ecology that sustains us.

We can't experience the luxuries of our modern lives based only on what our family, friends, and people like us produce. Self-interest at the expense of the common interest is self-defeating.

Once we remember we survive daily based on the contributions of many people we will never know—the well-being of all of us becomes as important as our own well-being.

Why must we remember now?

We face global challenges beyond the capacity of self-interest to mitigate:

1. **Climate crisis** – we are within 15 years of exceeding the average global surface temperature increase since 1850 of 1.5 degrees Celsius. This level of warming is the beginning of an extinction-level event.

2. **Income, wealth & global resource inequality** is destroying democratic institutions and destabilizing national governments, which is leading to severe polarization and mass migration of under-resourced populations

3. **Nuclear weapons proliferation** – Iran will be the next nation to obtain nuclear weapons because their most powerful enemies (Israel and USA) have nuclear weapons. This is not new. India responded similarly to Pakistan, obtaining nuclear weapons.

4. **Technological disruption** due to automation and artificial intelligence is displacing low-skilled labor and, ultimately, highly skilled labor. Since technology is owned by wealthy elites through control of multi-national corporations, income and wealth inequality is exacerbated because income from automated productivity goes to the owners of technology. Masses of people are becoming economically irrelevant.

While our earth is abundant, self-interest has rendered humanity impotent in the face of severe inequality and resource deprivation.

Yet we still have a choice, if only we remember who we are.

Just the facts[*]

For 10,000 years, the average global surface temperature remained stable within 1° Celsius.

The stable temperature produced consistent weather patterns that allowed humanity to develop farming. Farming allowed humanity to produce surplus food that supported faster population growth, trade, and ultimately modern civilization.

Carbon, methane, and other greenhouse gas emissions in the atmosphere cause global warming.

For every 1,000 $GtCO_2$ of carbon in the atmosphere, the average global surface temperature increases by 0.45°C.

Since 1850 (about the beginning of the Industrial Revolution), the accumulated carbon pollution in the atmosphere has been approximately 2,390 $GtCO_2$.

Currently, human activity is putting approximately 60 $GtCO_2$ of carbon pollution into the atmosphere per year.

---

[*] The source of the data cited here is the scientific basis of the Summary for Policymakers from the UN's 6th Intergovernmental Panel on Climate Change (IPCC).

All 195 member nations of the IPCC have endorsed the findings of the report.

The Summary for Policymakers is 42 pages long (the whole report is almost 4,000 pages long).

Here is the link for your review:
https://www.ipcc.ch/report/ar6/wg1/#SPM

Despite all the talk about limiting greenhouse gas pollution, the amount of carbon pollution is increasing each year.

The 60-year average yearly increase in carbon pollution is 1.61%.

The 10-year average yearly increase in carbon pollution is 2.4%.

The 30-year projected average yearly increase in carbon pollution is 3.5%.

We have all noticed the proliferation of extreme weather events in recent years. Huge forest fires throughout the western and Pacific northwestern US, Greece, and Australia. Torrential rainfalls and flooding in Tennessee, Germany, Belgium, New York, New Jersey, and Connecticut. Tropical storms are escalating into category 4 hurricanes in Asia and the Gulf of Mexico. Severe heat waves bring 115°F weather to Portland, Seattle, and as far north as Saskatchewan (Canada). The rate of extreme weather events has tripled since the 1980s.

All these extreme weather events are due to global average surface temperature exceeding the historical standard deviation of 1^0Celsius, and increasing to 1.07°C since 1850.

We currently have more carbon in our atmosphere than the earth has experienced in 800,000 years.

By comparison, the last ice age ended 15,000 years ago.

The rate of global warming is accelerating due to positive feedback loops, such as the melting of the polar ice caps. The United Nations climate scientists estimate average global surface temperature increase will reach 1.5°C between 2030 and 2040.

At 1.5°C, the rate and intensity of extreme weather events will be unprecedented in the historical observational record.

And if you think we have plenty of time to reverse the greenhouse emissions in the atmosphere causing global warming, in order to give the planet a 50 percent chance not to exceed 1.5°C by 2050, our 30-year average annual carbon emissions cannot exceed 16.67 $GtCO_2$.

That is 72 percent less than our current annual carbon pollution of 60 $GtCO_2$ per year for the next 30 years.

The climate crisis is real, and it is here. The economy exists within the ecology. Get educated on what sustains human life.

How Wealthy Elites Chose to Betray the American Working Class

Greed is not new, but previous generations learned hard lessons about the perils of consolidating wealth in too few hands. The Gilded Age led to the Great Depression of the 1890s, and the roaring '20s led to the stock market crash of 1929 and the Great Depression of the 1930s.

Out of necessity, FDR instituted the new deal framework that reined in excessive financial speculation and established the modern social safety net. Add in expanded access to college education and home ownership in the 1950s, and you have the largest and most prosperous working class in global history.

Then Lewis Powell wrote the Powell memo to the US Chamber of Commerce in 1971 as a call to arms for American corporations to co-opt the media, university system, and the government to advance the interest of American corporations. Powell was appointed to the Supreme Court in 1972 while major corporations deployed the strategy outlined in the memo.

American wealthy elites learned from 1950 – 1970 broad-based prosperity was too expensive because they could not control the American people. By 1970, working-class Americans were transforming the country through the civil rights movement, anti-war movement, equal rights movement, and were attempting to organize a poor man's march on Washington DC when Dr. Martin Luther King Jr. was assassinated in Memphis.

Yet the wealthy elites knew the lessons of previous efforts to consolidate wealth in too few hands had led to ruinous depressions. Their solution was to make wealth insulated from depressions by privatizing profits and socializing losses.

First, President Reagan dealt a death knell to the American Labor movement by firing the striking air traffic controllers in 1981. Then President H.W. Bush negotiated, and President Bill Clinton supported the ratification of the North American Free Trade Agreement (NAFTA), which de-industrialized America by off-shoring millions of manufacturing jobs.

By the late 1990s, Wall Street forced Congress to repeal Glass-Steagall by merging Travelers Insurance with Citibank, which gave Congress one year to break up the largest financial services company in the world. Congress caved and repealed Glass-Steagall. Then in the lame-duck Congress at the end of Bill Clinton's presidency, Congress passed sweeping legislation deregulating complex financial instruments.

Wall Street then utilized complex collateralized debt obligations rated AAA by captive credit rating agencies to loot restricted institutional investors such as pension funds, life insurance companies, and municipal investors, and prey on unsuspecting residential mortgage holders. By the end of 2006, institutional investors stopped buying the mis-rated securities, which trapped homeowners in rapidly escalating adjustable-rate mortgages and destroyed the investment banks that got caught holding trillions of dollars of worthless securities.

Some banks hedged their fraudulent investments with

credit default swaps that bankrupted AIG (the world's largest insurance company). Wall Street's exit strategy was "too big to fail," perfectly executed by former Goldman CEO Hank Paulsen, who was selected to be W's perfectly timed Treasury Secretary.

The great recession protected wealth while millions of Americans lost jobs, homes, pensions, and retirement savings. No major banker went to jail because President Clinton made the complex financial instruments legal, and President Obama refused to use the RICO laws to prosecute the rampant fraud on the American people (Google "William K Black").

The method was replicated with the COVID-19 pandemic. The CARES Act gave temporary support to individuals and small businesses (which expired by August 2020) while authorizing the Federal Reserve to "invest" $4.25 trillion in large multi-national corporations. By year-end, 2020 GDP contracted 3.5 percent, but the Dow Jones Industrial Average index increased 7.2 percent, S&P 500 increased 16.3 percent, Russell 2000 increased 18.4 percent, and the Nasdaq Composite increased 43.9 percent. US billionaires' net worth increased by over a trillion dollars, while 30 percent of all small businesses failed and never reopened, and workers with annual wages of $26,000 or less lost ten million jobs.

Thankfully, the American working class is fighting back. For the first time in 40 years, there are multiple strikes ongoing across America involving thousands of workers in deep red (Alabama) and dark blue (New York) states. The great resignation has totaled over 47 million workers with monthly recurring all-time records in August 2021 (4.2 million workers quit) and September 2021 (4.3 million) and continuing in March 2022 (4.5 million workers quit).

Now is the time for each of us to decide with whom do we stand?

I stand with the working class.

VOLUME 5

Impetus to a New Paradigm

When money no longer exists

What separates you and me from the Walton family, Bill Gates, Warren Buffet, and every extremely wealthy person on the planet? Cash...specifically, the huge accumulation of cash. And with their huge accumulation of cash comes influence and control over an extraordinary portion of our finite resources.

Now imagine an economy where money no longer exists. We no longer compete to accumulate cash in order to access the resources we need to sustain ourselves and our families. If we all have the same claim on our finite resources, we all have an interest in making sure our access provides for a high-quality, mutually fulfilling, and sustainable living condition. Individual accumulation of resources is no longer necessary because everyone will have all the resources we can use to reach our full potential.

From our birth, we will have full access to the complete body of human knowledge. We will be free to pursue our educational passions and select our vocations based solely on our highest aspirations. Human innovation will be unleashed to the maximum potential because it is informed by the accumulation of human knowledge and unhindered by limited access to our finite resources. Since our quality of life will be a function of our total contributions, all of us will be motivated to add new contributions to improve our living conditions. Imagine how productive we each could be if we all worked in the field of our highest, well-informed aspirations? But what about the wide range of mundane vocations necessary for modern living? This is the appropriate application for automated technology. By maximizing the use of automated technology to fulfill the myriad of mundane functions, each of us is free to turn our focus on the areas of our maximum contribution.

The latest innovations are no longer exclusive to those few who can afford to pay for them. All goods and services are provided to the highest level of quality and efficiency in order to maximize our contribution to our mutual well-being and minimize waste.

A successful life will no longer be measured by who accumulates more resources for themselves but by who contributes most to the quality of life of the global community.

What if

Remember playing "what if" as a child? What if you had a million dollars? What if you could live forever? I used to spend a lot of time daydreaming about what if. Today, as I consider my life, I now wonder what if my life was free from the constraints of money? The more I think about the impact money has on my life, the more I realize I am a slave to the need for money.

Virtually everything I know, everything I do, everywhere I go, everything I eat, and everywhere I sleep...is all determined by money. It has always been this way.

Yet, in many ways, I'm a very blessed man. I was born and raised in the richest country in the world. I was provided a fantastic private school education. I entered my adulthood at a time when opportunities were opening to aspiring adults from an expanding range of ethnic, racial, and gender backgrounds. My chosen career came from among a wide range of choices, informed by extensive access to our accumulated knowledge. Despite all of these advantages, virtually every choice I have made was a function of money.

What if we all were free to make choices not constrained by the need for money? Let that thought sink in.

Imagine being born in a world where global resources were managed to maximize sustainability and minimize waste. Technology and innovation are deployed to produce the best products and services based on the accumulation of human knowledge. Automation is maximized to provide all the mundane, repetitive processes and services necessary for modern life, freeing each of us to focus our energies on pursuing our highest vocational aspirations. Every person would have access to a comprehensive education where the goal is scholarship, not wealth. In such a world, a virtuous life would be measured by how each of us contributes to the well-being of all of us.

Sounds like Utopia?

Actually, this is what freedom feels like. Free people are empowered to reach their full potential. Slaves are constrained from reaching their full potential for the benefit of their masters. As we examine our lives today, how many of us can truly say we are free?

Eternity within

At the heart of everything we touch, everything we experience, and even who we are...is energy.

From the first spark of energy received from the merging of a sperm cell with an egg cell, our bodies have been fueled by energy that sustains it until the energy leaves our body at death.

The existence empowered by energy replicates in everything we transfer energy to...

A flower, a novel, a child, a nation.

The more thoughtful energy we invest in the things and people who touch our lives, the more we contribute to creating a world in our image. Here we replicate the gift of divine creation.

Scripture teaches we were created in the Divine's image. We know all things true about the Divine have always been true because the Divine is eternal and never changes. What about us is Divine, has always been true, and is not subject to change?

Our essential energy.

Now observe your life. That which you invest your energy blooms. And that which you ignore degrades until it can be energized into a new creation.

Realizing our divinity empowers us to shed our resignation of a world gone wrong and participate in the creation of a world worth living in.

Tap into your eternity within and join the effort to make the world worthy of our progeny.

And Then She Awakes

Was it the random streak she happened to notice across the sky?

Or successfully jamming her brakes to avoid the car that suddenly stopped in front of her and realizing her mechanic just saved her life?

Or reading the label on her favorite coffee and noticing the beans were picked by indigenous people from a distant land?

Any of these reasons, or maybe the slow accumulation of experiences, finally crystallized into her new epiphany:

She is one participant in her life journey, fully realized by the choices of many actors.

Now what? Can I proceed to view my life as my own when it actually is not?

Can I look at people I do not know as strangers when their choices are contributing to my well-being?

Does it make sense to pray for my nation alone when so many influencers to my life's journey live beyond our national borders?

No.

I can no longer view my life as I did before.

"Us" used to be very clear: myself, my family, my friends, my employer, my nation, my religion, and my preferences. And "Them" were not "Us."

Yet how can my mechanic be a "Them" when he saved my life?

As I consider the food I eat, the clothes I wear, the bed I sleep on each night, and the home that provides me shelter, I realize virtually everything I utilize to support my wellness was produced by people and with resources from places around our world.

Can all these people who I rely on daily remain beyond my thoughts and concerns?

No.

I must acknowledge my "Us" has expanded to include almost everyone.

And who remains beyond "Us?"

Anyone who hurts "Us."

Now, I am finally awake.

Us

There is no more euphoric feeling we experience in this life than when we are One.

Physically our oneness culminates as an orgasm.

Emotionally our oneness manifests as love.

Spiritually our oneness is realized as fulfillment.

And when all aspects of our reality align, the illusion of our independent, separate existence disappears.

We wake up from the dream that encouraged us to forget.

We transcend the limitations of this thing called life.

Our energy flows unimpeded by time or space.

We are one with each other.

We are one with Source.

We are empowered to create.

Finally...we remember who we are.

An Alternative to Money

Money is a very efficient medium of exchange compared to barter. The problem with money is it ties access to resources based solely on possessing it. The more money you have, the more resources you can control.

Accordingly, money is amoral because it is indifferent to the need for resources. The existence of money necessitates scarcity in the availability of resources by allowing a few people to possess control over enormous resources, leaving most people on earth resource-deprived.

What then is a meaningful alternative? To answer this question, I need to review a few indisputable facts:

We share one planet, which produces a finite amount of natural resources that sustains all of us.

Technological advances leverage our natural resources to produce a finite amount of finished goods and services.

If each person is empowered to possess as many resources as they are able to accumulate, there will never be enough resources for everyone.

This old paradigm is not sustainable.

We face a moment where humanity must reach for the next stage of our social evolution.

Consider...

If all people have access to the accumulation of human knowledge, they will possess the necessary information to identify their unique talents and perfect their unique skills in order to maximize their individual productivity.

If humanity guarantees access to the resources each person can use to reach and maintain their full potential, there would be no need to accumulate excess resources for ourselves.

Eliminating money and guaranteeing access to resources eliminates price and quality differentiation of goods and services, which occur today to allow fortunes to be made on affordable, sub-standard goods and services.

If all goods and services are designed to provide the highest quality possible, enormous resources will be saved by eliminating repetitive consumption, planned obsolescence, and other economic inefficiencies common to the current global economy. Wellness will be optimized for all people.

If we shift from an ownership relationship with resources to a stewardship relationship, we will maximize utilization and minimize waste.

Currently, we possess resources that are idle until we are ready to use them. In a sustainable society, sophisticated use-share systems can be innovated that would allow people to reserve resources for when they are needed. This would make resources available on demand.

Accordingly, access to resources will be based on what we can USE...no more and no less.

Waste and gluttony will be global security violations.

Sustainability will be restored and maintained through a system of global resource management informed by open-sourced access to the accumulation of human knowledge.

This can be our future reality if we have the courage to consider an alternative to money.

When Less is Truly More

Wisdom teaches us the only thing we actually know is the truth we are finally ready to realize.

Everything else is opinion tainted by a lifetime of subjective experiences.

As such, the more we know, the more we realize we don't know.

Yet through this epiphany, we discover authentic humility, which slows judgment long enough to create space for more truth to be understood.

The Matrix Exposed

If you believe you are a stone-cold realist who sees truth as it actually is, consider...

Are you free?

Free to choose your life's vocation unconstrained by how much money you will make?

Free to spend your non-working and sleeping time doing the activities you enjoy most?

Free to invest the time you need to build healthy relationships with family and friends?

Are you independent?

How much of what you do is reliant on what other people have done?

Of all the words you have thought or spoken, which ones did you create?

How much of what you need to survive daily do you (or can you) produce?

Does self-interest really serve you?

Every hurdle you face to all you desire is due to other people advancing their own self-interest.

Is competition really a good thing?

Every person you defeat in the competition for resources is a person you may need to rely on for the goods and services that support you.

The conventional wisdom inherent to each of these bolded questions is the Matrix.

Truth resides in your responses.

A Virtuous Cycle

Red blood cells deliver oxygen to all parts of our body, allowing us to function, which provides the environment red blood cells need to survive.

When we exhale, we release carbon dioxide into the air. Trees absorb the carbon and use it for photosynthesis, which produces food as it cleans the air we breathe.

For over 10,000 years, the global average temperature stabilized to within 1 degree Celsius. The stable temperature produced predictable weather that allowed humanity to evolve beyond hunter-gatherer nomadic communities to develop farming, produce surplus food and products for trade, and create modern civilization. This period that cultivated extraordinary human development is called the Holocene.

In our modern society, each of us contributes our most marketable skill in exchange for money, which we use to purchase all the goods and services we need to sustain ourselves.

This is the pattern of existence in nature...

A virtuous cycle of interdependence and mutual fulfillment.

Yet since the beginning of the Industrial Revolution (1850), human productivity has raised global average temperatures beyond 1 degree Celsius. As human activities pushed our ecology out of the Holocene, the impact on biodiversity has been catastrophic, with species extinctions exceeding a thousand times the normal rate.

Today, we are within one average lifespan of depleting our soil of essential nutrients, Savannization of tropical forests, ocean acidification, and melting of the polar icecaps.

The virtuous cycle has been broken.

We now face a choice: innovate a modern economic system that supports ecological sustainability or participate in the sixth mass extinction event.

Anatomy of a Purpose

Existence is comprised of energy manipulating matter.

Balance is the necessary condition for flow to occur.

Flow is the essential function of energy.

Love is the unimpeded flow of energy.

Wellness is the balance of food, water, rest, and exercise.

Sustainability is the balance of giving and receiving.

Alignment is the balance of experience with wisdom.

Fulfillment is the *alignment* of *sustainable love* with *wellness*.

Purpose is the *fulfillment* of our *existence*.

What I want

I want to celebrate my sovereignty within the context of our universal oneness...

In alignment...

In balance...

In sustainable perpetual abundance.

Why?

Because this is the Truth about who we are.

When No One's Left to Blame

I was so certain it was all their fault.

We all said it. We all knew it. And we gladly made them pay.

Yet the next day, I woke, and nothing was better.

So I was handed another victim...I hurt another target... and still, nothing had changed.

When they offered me a new scapegoat, there was no joy in making them pay.

I had finally noticed this stranger looked no better off than me.

He had been lied to...just like me.

She hungered for justice...just like me.

They were suffering...just like me.

At last, I realized...they were just like me.

Where we are

We are immersed in a perfect storm of transformative events.

A global pandemic,

the climate crisis,

lack of trust in democratic institutions (government, media, experts, corporations, each other...),

severe wealth & income inequality,

technological disruption, and

nuclear proliferation.

Yet I remain hopeful.

Evolutionary metamorphosis involves catastrophic change...

...that begins with the collapse of what was,

...and ends with the birth of what shall be.

When we emerge, we will have evolved into a new paradigm of consciousness where sovereignty and unity are aligned.

A Path to Sustainability

COP26 is merely the start of our transformation to a 21st-century sustainable economy. As it stands now, we have non-binding commitments to cut GHG emissions by 50 percent by 2030.

Here is what we need:

Binding commitments to tie net-zero transition to a peak global average surface temperature increase of 1.5°C.

Graduated carbon pricing of $100 per ton by 2025, $125 by 2030, and $150 by 2035 & thereafter.

Acknowledgment of the carbon budget from 1850 to peak temperature increase of 1.5°C.

A retroactive carbon price of $50 per ton was charged to the wealthy nations who benefited most from the 2,400 $GtCO_2$ of carbon pollution emitted since 1850. This $120 trillion will initially capitalize the Global Net Zero Transition Fund. Future carbon pricing proceeds will be injected directly into the Fund.

Establish a fossil fuel-stranded assets regime that will tie future subsidies and stranded assets compensation to invest in scaling up renewable energy power generation, including new sources such as green hydrogen and ammonia.

Establish a Leap Frog power generation program for India, China, and the emerging world funded by the Global Net Zero Transition Fund. Leap Frog means increasing energy production from carbon-free, sustainable energy sources.

Require all businesses to disclose a decarbonization transition plan tied to the peak temperature increase of 1.5°C and inclusive of 95 percent of scope 1, scope 2, and scope three emissions by 2025 or face 2030 carbon pricing fees.

Establish a global anti-profiteering regime capping Return on Investment for Net Zero Transition activities. We will not succeed if investors can impose economic rents at every stress point.

Can we do it?

Yes...

If enough of us convince the wealthy elites, they will not escape the price of inaction.

The Tribe is Gathering

Like-minded, peace-loving, freedom-seeking people are finding each other by filtering out the trolls, liars, manipulators, propagandists, narcissists, and hoarders from our physical and virtual networks.

The problem is the powers that be demand control of everyone and everything. Therefore, gathering in our own social networks is not enough. We must build a critical mass of people willing to stop feeding the beast who lives on the work we produce.

The first step to building the critical mass is to reject the labels we have been given that encourage us to hate each other.

All identity-based labels obscure our shared humanity.

Marketing labels, sports affiliations, business associations, community/state/national identification, political classifications, religious/gender/racial/pronoun and cultural identifiers all should be set aside so we can finally accept and mutually respect the sovereignty of each of us.

We set these labels aside not to deny our own unique identities but to create solidarity on the basis we each are empowered to make our own choices.

Rejecting our labels reveals who benefits from the divisiveness dominating our societies.

Like the sunrise after a very dark night, each of us will see how completely we have been distracted by manufactured consent.

Nothing in nature lives independently.

Freedom is a virtue because having it supports a life worth living.

As our tribe gathers, we reclaim our sovereignty by networking globally while living and buying as locally as possible.

An Open Letter regarding the War in Ukraine

Dear friend,

I have been thinking about our discussion regarding the War in Ukraine. I believe we have an understanding of where we each stand in regard to the conflict, but I will restate our positions for the sake of clarity.

Your view is Russia initiated the escalation of the conflict by launching a military attack on Ukraine. As the aggressor, you hold Russia responsible for the humanitarian crisis occurring in Ukraine. You are aware there are historical events that may have contributed to the current conflict, but no historical event justifies Russia's military attack on Ukraine. Your hope is the Russians will overthrow Putin and his government apparatus.

My view is the United States instigated the conflict by breaking the verbal assurance given by Presidents H.W Bush & Clinton provided to Gorbachev and Yeltsin to limit NATO's eastern expansion beyond the unified Germany. In exchange for the private assurance (the same type of assurance that resolved the Cuban Missile crisis), the former U.S.S.R agreed to support unified Germany's admission into NATO and the peaceful dismantling of the Soviet Union. The Soviet Union executed the dissolution, including gathering the nuclear arsenal from the satellite states to Russia and supporting German re-unification and entry into NATO. At the time of the private assurance, there were ten former Warsaw Pact nations that comprised the security buffer between Europe and Russia.

Starting in the late 1990s, NATO began the practice of adding former Warsaw Pact nations. Currently, seven of the original ten countries have been admitted into NATO. With each new addition, the American Military Industrial complex modernized the former Warsaw Pact countries to NATO grade military weaponry, including some with ballistic missiles capable of striking Russia. With each new NATO addition, Russia lodged vigorous complaints and threats of military escalation to restore the security buffer between Europe and Russia.

One month after the beginning of the War in Ukraine, Russia stated they would end the war and withdraw from Ukraine if the following four conditions were met:

> Ukraine signs a neutrality agreement that would bar it from entering NATO
> Recognize Crimea as Russian
> Recognize Luhansk and Donetsk as independent
> Agree to a mutual cease-fire

Ukraine has indicated it would no longer pursue admission into NATO and are open to a neutrality agreement. Ukraine has asked America to empower them in the negotiations by tying the removal of international economic sanctions to the Ukrainian negotiated peace agreement. Thus far, we have refused.

We are at a stalemate in our discussion. We must agree to

disagree.

What remains is the question of regime change in Russia, which President Biden acknowledged on his recent European trip. On this issue, I believe America, even as the sole super-power, is over her skis.

The world is watching as we have weaponized economic sanctions beyond any historical reference point to overthrow a G20 & permanent UN Security Council nation for reasons we have been guilty of many times over. This is the latest example of how we have chosen to lead the world...as a petulant nation that has sacrificed our moral standing on the iron altar of brute force. This approach has only hardened our enemies and given our friends pause because we have been arrogant enough to affirm many times our America-first foreign policy agenda. Given the opportunity, the EU, UK, Canada, and other "friends" may jump at the chance to break free of our yoke.

Our overplay of the War in Ukraine by revealing the intent to overthrow Putin may induce China to partner with Russia to establish an alternative to the Swift exchange system. This would be the opening needed to establish a new international currency of trade. Russia already requires the EU to pay for oil and natural gas in Rubles. Saudi Arabia is not accepting President Biden's calls and has demonstrated an interest in using a different currency for OPEC oil transactions. If an alternative exchange system is organized with China, Russia, and potentially OPEC, this will give our "friends" a legitimate alternative to our American-dominated SWIFT system. My point here is force has a limit when you are interdependent on your "subordinate" nation-state partners.

At the heart of the matter, my worldview is not political. My worldview is spiritual. When I look at the US-dominated prevailing narrative over the last 50 years, we are persistently given an enemy to focus our hate on...the U.S.S.R, Iran, terrorists (including Iraq & Afghanistan), North Korea, and now Putin (Russia). Each of our "enemies" had verifiable facts that paint a foggier picture than the clear-cut vilification story we are fed by the media and our government.

The pre-curser to the Cuban Missile crisis was the United States deployed ballistic missiles in Turkey. The Soviets responded by installing the missiles in Cuba. We then escalated to a threatened nuclear exchange because nuclear-armed ballistic missiles deployed in Cuba violated the American security buffer. The crisis was resolved when America gave the Russians a private assurance to quietly remove the ballistic missiles from Turkey six months after the Soviets agreed to remove their missiles from Cuba.

In 1953, the United States orchestrated the overthrow of the democratically elected leader of Iran in order to protect British oil interests. Prime Minister Mosaddegh was ousted in favor of a pro-American government ultimately led by the Shah of Iran. By the 1970s, after years of brutal treatment of dissidents, the Shah was overthrown by the Iranian Revolutionary Army. The new Iranian government's first official act was to endorse the seizure of the American embassy in Tehran. When the US arranged a safe asylum in the Philippines for the Shah, after seriously considering providing safe harbor in the US, negotiations for the hostages' release broke down. After Iran finally surrendered the hostages at the start of the Reagan administration, we punished the Iranians by arming the Iraqis with chemical and biological weapons in the Iraqi-Iranian War of the 1980s, effectively killing hundreds of thousands of Iranians.

America's role in the proliferation of terrorism continued in the Soviet-Afghanistan War of the 1980s. Here an Islamic militia called the Mujaheddin was armed and trained by the US to embroil the Soviets in a quagmire conflict that effectively broke the morale of the Soviet military as they were forced to retreat back to the Soviet Union.

Iraq, emboldened by its success at repelling the much larger Iranian military in the Iraqi-Iranian War, turned its attention to Kuwait, where it claimed the country as the 13th Iraqi state. The brazen act of aggression sent shock waves around the globe based on the fear the Iraqis may extend their aggression to include Saudi Arabia. To repel this threat on the Arabian peninsula, Osama Bin Laden offered the Saudi Royal Family to re-enlist the victorious Mujaheddin to repel the Iraqi forces back out of Kuwait. The offer was made to protect the home of Mecca, the Islamic holy of the holies, from Iraqi infidels. Instead, the Saudi Royal Family made a deal with America to repel Iraq from Kuwait in exchange for a number of permanent US military bases in Saudi Arabia. The establishment of permanent US military bases in Saudi Arabia, home of Mecca, is the cited basis for Bin Laden's Fatwa against America and the Saudi Royal Family that ultimately led to the terrorist attacks on 9/11.

Many countries have aspirations of developing nuclear

weapons. Libya established a WMD program in the 1990s. After years of US-led pressure, in 2004, Libyan President Muammar Gaddafi agreed to dismantle the country's nuclear weapons program. By 2011, a US-led NATO attack on Libya supported a successful uprising to overthrow the government of Muammar Gaddafi, who was publicly tortured and murdered in October 2011. Is it a mere coincidence North Korea has since accelerated its nuclear weapons program to include multiple launch attempts?

My point here is to illuminate geopolitical motivations are far more complicated than the black and white vilification narratives propagated by the media and our government. Manufactured consent is a virulent cancer to any healthy democracy. We must resist first by rejecting the prevailing narrative, then seek the facts as best as we can.

Epilogue

How did we arrive at a time where we know something is deeply wrong with our society and yet have no idea what it is or how to fix it?

We arrived here by deferring our sense of truth to external influences...social virtues, leaders, experts, and narratives.

Yet we can reclaim our personal sovereignty by quieting the external noise and trusting the inner voice of our highest selves.

Here lies the steeped wisdom learned from our lived experiences.

Here we see what actually works.

Here we discover that all our answers to living a fulfilled life begin by looking in the mirror.

How can I make a difference when everything seems too big to change?

I can acknowledge that change begins with me.

Starting with a sober assessment of how I survive each day, I can finally shed the I centered lens of our social conditioning.

I can remember my existence is interdependent on humanity and the natural ecology that sustains me.

By remembering our natural interdependence, we are able to see why things are so desperately wrong and how we are able to do our part in making them right.

Category Index

Current Events:

Economics:

Personal Growth:

Starting points of reference

The following references display a range of sources I use to expand my consideration beyond the standard narrative.

Daniel Quinn
- The Story of B
- Ishmael

Paul Hawken
- Regeneration

Clifford D. Conner
- The Tragedy of American Science

Paul Behrens
- The Best of Times, The Worst of Times – Futures from the Frontiers of Climate Science

Kim Stanley Robinson
- The Ministry of the Future

Yuval Noah Harari (https://www.ynharari.com/)
- Sapiens
- Homo Deus
- 21 Lessons for the 21st Century

Tim Jackson
- Prosperity Without Growth – Foundations for the Economy of Tomorrow
- Post Growth – Life After Capitalism

Yanis Varoufakis (https://www.yanisvaroufakis.eu/)
- Diem 25 (https://diem25.org/what-is-diem25/)
- Another Now
- Adults in the Room

Heather Heying & Bret Weinstein
- A Hunter Gatherer's Guide to the 21st Century

Dr. Martin Luther King Jr.
- Letter from Birmingham Jail

Chris Hedges
- America: The Farewell Tour
- The Politics of Cultural Despair (https://youtu.be/GxSN4ip_F6M)

Richard Wolff (https://www.rdwolff.com/)
- Democracy at Work
  (https://www.patreon.com/m/880018/posts)
- The System is the Sickness

Anne Case and Angus Deaton
- Deaths of Despair and the future of capitalism

Daniel Markovits
- The Meritocracy Trap

Stephanie Kelton
- The Deficit Myth

James Baldwin
- The Fire Next Time

Peter Joseph (https://www.peterjoseph.info/)
- The Zeitgeist Movement – https://thezeitgeistmovement.com
- The New Human Rights Movement
- InterReflections
  (https://www.interreflectionsmovie.com/about)

Sir David Attenborough
- A Life on Our Planet (Documentary)
- Breaking Boundaries – The Science of Our Planet (Documentary)

Pope Francis (Encyclicals)
- Fratelli Tutti (2020)
- Laudato si (2015)

Noam Chomsky and Marv Waterstone
- Consequences of Capitalism

T. Colin Campbell
- The China Study

James Nestor
- Breathe

Joshua Fields Millburn and Ryan Nicodemus
- Essential – Essays by the Minimalists

Helen Russell
- The Year of Living Danishly

Matt Kahn
- Whatever arises, Love That: A Love Revolution
- The Universe Always Has a Plan
- All for Love

Paramahansa Yogananda
- Autobiography of a Yogi

Richard L. Haight
- The Unbound Soul: A Visionary Guide to Spiritual Transformation and Enlightenment

Marianne Williamson
- A Politics of Love

Eckhart Tolle
- The New Earth: Awakening your life's purpose

Humanity's Team

- https://www.humanitysteam.org/oneness-declarations
  #English

Enjoy!

About Atmosphere Press

Atmosphere Press is an independent, full-service publisher for excellent books in all genres and for all audiences. Learn more about what we do at atmospherepress.com.

We encourage you to check out some of Atmosphere's latest releases, which are available at Amazon.com and via order from your local bookstore:

The Great Unfixables, by Neil Taylor

Soused at the Manor House, by Brian Crawford

Portal or Hole: Meditations on Art, Religion, Race And The Pandemic, by Pamela M. Connell

A Walk Through the Wilderness, by Dan Conger

The House at 104: Memoir of a Childhood, by Anne Hegnauer

A Short History of Newton Hall, Chester, by Chris Fozzard

Serial Love: When Happily Ever After... Isn't, by Kathy Kay

Sit-Ins, Drive-Ins and Uncle Sam, by Bill Slawter

Black Water and Tulips, by Sara Mansfield Taber

Ghosted: Dating & Other Paramoural Experiences, by Jana Eisenstein

Walking with Fay: My Mother's Uncharted Path into Dementia, by Carolyn Testa

FLAWED HOUSES of FOUR SEASONS, by James Morris

Word for New Weddings, by David Glusker and Thom Blackstone

It's Really All about Collaboration and Creativity! A Textbook and Self-Study Guide for the Instrumental Music Ensemble Conductor, by John F. Colson

A Life of Obstructions, by Rob Penfield

Troubled Skies Over Quaker Hill: A Search for the Truth, by Lessie Auletti

About the Author

I was born and raised in the Bronx, NY. I had a very happy childhood with my brother, Ruben, and my mother, Andrea. I graduated from Cardinal Spellman High School, then served four years of active duty in the US Army as a member of NATO. I attended college in Houston, Texas, and graduate school in Connecticut. My career began with a one-year commitment as a FEMA Disaster Assistance Loan Officer primarily assigned to the Northridge earthquake declared natural disaster. I went on to build a successful career as a business banker but found my calling in climate risk mitigation. I am happily married to Nikole and live in a nature preserve community on the Oregon Pacific coast. I am a life learner who draws strength and inspiration from my connection with humanity and the natural environment that sustains us.

A few fun facts about me:

My first world series occurred in 1975, where I rooted for Carlton Fisk and the Boston Red Sox. We lost to Pete Rose and the Big Red Machine (Cincinnati Reds). I became a lifelong New York Yankee fan the following season.

At 20, I drove and loaded an M-1 Tank and participated in night gunnery exercises.

I served as an Olympic Games volunteer for the 1996 Atlanta Olympic Games. I worked at the Boxing venue.

On vacation in Nicaragua, I had the pleasure of riding a

horse as she swam across a stream...priceless!

In 2021, I completed my personal Manifest Destiny by living in the Bronx, Atlanta, Houston, Phoenix, Washougal (WA), and now Otis, OR.

My inspiration for writing Onward, At Last:

I was a true believer in the American Dream. A US Army veteran who enlisted to kill or be killed to protect the American way of life. I achieved the ideal American middle-class life...and yet I felt completely disillusioned and physically on the path to a stroke at the age of 40.

My burning question: Why am I not happy?

The commentaries in *Onward, At Last*, reveal the lessons I learned on my path to fulfillment. In the nadir of my personal journey, I discovered the truth I had come to realize was far more a function of my experience than the explanations society provides.